First Published in 2020 by

Christian World Imprints
Christian Publishing & Books from India
C-3, Wazirpur Industrial Area
Delhi-110052
cwidelhi2017@gmail.com
www.ChristianWorldImprints.com
Phone: +91 11 41526079

ISBN: 978-93-5148-483-7 (HB)
ISBN: 978-93-5148-484-4 (PB)

Printed in India.

Contents

Foreword

During the first half of the 20th century, within a span of barely 50 years, the whole Mizo community embraced Christianity. This would certainly be an extraordinary phenomenon in the history of the world-wide Christianity. It has often been considered that the rapid growth of the Church in Mizoram was the impact of non-intermittent phases of gospel revivals which took place in distinctive forms at particular time intervals in this part of Northeast India. These revivals with their overwhelming vigor and dynamic energized and vivified the life and ministry of the Church in an unfathomable scale. One of such revivals in recent times was the so-called El-Bethel Revival which took place in the middle of 1990s and made continuing impact on the life of the church in Mizoram for decades that followed. The El-Bethel Revival was spearheaded by a gifted and committed speaker, a lay itinerant evangelist K. Lalhmingliana.

I am very happy that my colleague, Rev. Lalchawimawia, an Associate Professor (Homiletics) at the Aizawl Theological College is publishing his M.Th. thesis in a book form in which he carefully analyzes the El-Bethel Revival phenomenon with standard academic research principles. In this book the author brings out insightful findings as a result of his careful and critical study on the key person, namely, K. Lalhmingliana who stood behind this great revival; his sermons (type and theology); the organization and function of his evangelistic team; and the influence that this revival had upon the life of the people and the church.

I feel privileged and honored to write a foreword to this book and it is my sincere prayer that the author will carry on a fruitful ministry and that each and every reader will be blessed through encountering with this valuable book.

Rev. Prof. Vanlalnghaka Ralte
Principal
Aizawl Theological College

Acknowlegement

First of all, I am grateful to God, who so generously called me into the Pastoral ministry and led me to undertake this Master of Theology in Christian Ministry course. I express my deepest gratitude to God for His guidance, wisdom and strength during this study period.

I am thankful to Dr. G. Isaiah, who was not only my teacher and guide, but my Mentor, for his immense help not only in my studies, research work, but also in other ways in my life. I have been privileged to benefit from his encouragements, advice, and ready availability for consultation and suggestions.

I express my special thanks to El-Bethel Publication Board and Mizoram State Library staff for allowing me to use most of the documents for the success of this research.

I am very grateful to Prof. Vanlalnghaka Ralte, Principal, Aizawl Theological College, who is my former teacher and colleague in the theological education and ministry. It was very nice of him that he willingly accepts my humble request and wrote a wonderful foreword for my book in the midst of his busy schedule.

My gratitude will be incomplete if my beloved wife, Lalrammawii, my beloved Children Joan, Isaac, Judith, Ebenezer are left out. My wife and my children have always been taking care of me, always helped, provoked, and encouraged me even in midst of frustration during my two years study of this course.

This book in its original from is the thesis submitted to the Senate of Serampore College towards Master of Theology (MTh) degree and published it with permission from the Senate. The author is responsible for the contents, ideas and opinions expressed in the book. The title of the book is reframed to the present form for the purpose of publication.

Preface

The book, with a title *Introducing Evangelical Homiletics: An Indigenous Approach,* attempts to examine the evangelical preaching done by the independent preacher K. Lalhmingliana and his team called El-Bethel Evangelistic Team. It is an attempt to prove an assumption that the preaching of evangelical preacher is more attractive than that of the pastors and elders of the Presbyterian Church and has created negative attitudes between the preaching of El- Bethel Team and the elders and pastors.

The book is divided into six chapters including introduction and nature of studies in chapter. Chapter two introduces the formation of El-Bethel Team and the nature and functions of 'the camping of El-Bethel team' along with the biography of the Speaker K. Lalhmingliana it also study the El-Bethel camping organized by Chanmari and Dawrpui Vengthar Presbyterian churches.

Chapter three contains the themes and biblical text of the sermons, history of collections; classifications of the sermons along with the analysis of the five sermons are also included. Since K. Hminga was a revival preacher, most of the preaching was to revive the spiritual life of the people towards the love and care of the sinners with a new heart. The 'Theme' of the sermons directly related to social issues. Corresponding to the theme, he chose the Biblical Texts. Thus, the themes determine the Biblical text. K. Hminga seems to give more importance to the theme and the nature of his audience than the Biblical text of his sermon.

Chapter four is an appraisal of the homiletic structure and the illustrations of the sermons of K. Hminga. This chapter shows that there is no long introduction in his preaching. In the conclusion he mainly follows two types of conclusion one is exhortation and another one is summarization, short but appealing and convincing. K. Hminga used a variety of illustrations in his preaching to make the sermon interesting to illuminate the messages to the audience.

Chapter five is an attempt to study the major theology emphasized by K. Hminga to the Mizo people this includes, The Seeds of Faith, The Bethel Prayer, The Doctrine of the Holy Spirit and Ministry of the Church. They are very effective and favored by the people; it looks appropriate for the church and for ministry, the church needs to steer and study these theologies thoroughly.

Chapter six is the concluding chapter which consists of the analysis of the questionnaire, findings, hypothesis tested, and final conclusion. The creativity, commitment and thoughtfulness of K. Hminga and his Team enriched the church and helped the church move forward for the extension of the Kingdom of God. People did not reject the preaching of the Pastors and Elders, as a result of the preaching of K. Hminga and lot has restored many families to a better Christian family. Ecumenism was restored among the churches due to the ministry of El-Bethel Team.

Without the support, cooperation, and encouragements of numerous professors, family, church members, and friends, a study of this nature would have not been possible. They all deserve to be acknowledged for their part in making this book a reality. They all have a share in whatever contribution this research work has made in extending the Kingdom of God.

Abbreviations

AGP	Agape Gospel Puangtu
ATC	Aizawl Theological College
CPSC	Chanmari Pastorate Standing Committee
D.C	Deputy Commissioner
DVPSC	Dawrpui Vengthar Pastorate Standing Committee
EFBC	Evangelical Free Church of Burma
EFCI	Evangelical Free Church of India
ff.	Followings
Govt.	Government
H/o	Husband of
i/c	in charge
ICI	Independent Church of India
K.T.P	Kristian Thalai Pawl (Christian Youth Association)
MNF	Mizo National Front
NGOs	Non Government Organizations
No	Number
n. p	no page number
NRSV	New Revised Standard Version
N.T	New Testament
O.T	Old Testament

P.C	Presbyterian Church
RV	Rendezvous
SEC	Synod Executive Committee
Sl	Serial
S/o	Son of
SoF	Seeds of Faith
Sr.	Senior
SRC	Synod Revival Committee
SRS	Synod Revival Speaker
SSFC	Synod Social Front Committee
US	United States of America
Vol.	Volume
W/o	Wife of

Chapter 1

Introduction

Preaching is one of the earliest and main instruments for the propagation of the Gospels. There are various types and forms of preaching, among which, indigenous preaching also helps the church grow; meanwhile there are some advantage and disadvantage depending upon to the context of the people and churches. This is an attempt to study **Evangelical preaching- El-Bethel Team.**

The NATURE OF STUDY is by the following:

I. The Research Problem

A large part of the church members in Mizoram appear to be more attracted to the evangelical preaching ministry of El-Bethel team than the conventional preaching of the pastors and elders, and this calls for an evaluation of the preaching of the El-Bethel team speaker. The preaching was effective and revived the people enormously and it was considered as revival preaching since it was preached to the Christians to bring them back to God.

During the first half of this 20th century revival occurred four times in the Mizoram Presbyterian Church. The first revival came in 1906, the second in 1913, the third in 1919 and the fourth in 1935. In 1984, another great revival took place in Mizoram. Since then this kind of movement affects the atmosphere of the church. In some ways it is good for the church because it helps the church move forward. There is an increase in offering and attendance in the church services but it also has negative side. The mushrooming of self-style evangelists / lay preachers teams began to interfere in the smooth running of the preaching ministry of the pastor and the elders. These self-styled evangelists form teams, and compose their team names for identification and systematic function in their preaching ministry.

This has caused disturbance in the preaching ministry of the church. They move from place to place, village to village, church to church, denomination to denomination, and preach even on the streets. They became very influential and some members of the church often urge the church committees to invite them to the church to deliver sermons. This has become a hindrance for the church and also seems to be alarming to the church committee because it is not possible to refuse them at all. At the same time because they are not members of the church it has become difficult to invite them regularly. The church already has its own doctrines, traditions, structures and systematic programmes are arranged for the worship and preaching ministry. When the revival preachers are invited to deliver sermons they do not pay attention to the doctrine and the administrative setup of the church. At the same time the church benefits also: they revive the spiritual life of the people and really help in bringing back the backsliders in the church fellowship; and many of them started attend the daily early Morning Prayer service. Among these teams the El-Bethel Evangelical team is one of the most famous evangelistic teams in the (Mizoram) North East India. It was established in 1988 and the main speaker was K. Lalhmingliana.

Majority of the people of the church are more attracted by the preaching of the evangelists more than the preaching of the pastors and the elders. The value of the church worship service and attendance is decreasing and this has become a serious issue for the church. People began to turn away from the preaching ministry of the elders and the pastors, and turned to the preaching ministry of the El-Bethel team. C. Vanlallawma stated that:

> In the early part those who thirst in spirit run after and flocked to them, but the Presbyterian Church, the biggest church in Mizoram was to keep an eye upon the ministry and the teaching of K. Lalhmingliana, since large number of people were attracted and started to support his ministry, so there was no time even to decide for the church regarding caution or goodwill. Many of those who attended the El-Bethel Camp compared their life before and after the camp were like the difference of day and night. Their attitude to those who do not attend in the camp was negative and they look them that they are dry, and they encouraged and compelled them to attend in the camp. In this atmosphere the elders are budging, and the pastors are quiver. [1]

From the previous historical revival movements several kinds of schismatic groups appeared.[2] In the early stage because of this El-Bethel team movement, some misunderstanding has come up within the church members; some favour[3] and some do not. At the same time, the preaching and teaching revived the people and drew them toward Christ. Therefore, it is necessary to have an in-depth study of the preaching of K. Lalhmingliana the main speaker of the El-Bethel Team. Why does the preaching attract the people? Is it his ability to articulate a deep theological truth or indigenous terminology? Is it the type of sermon construction, or the illustrations, the content or the style of preaching? At the same time we need to know and study the reasons for the weakness of the preaching of the pastors and elders of established churches.

---

1 C. Vanlallawma, *Bethel Revival and Lausanne Thuthlung* (Aizawl: Lengchhawn Press, 1990), 6.

2 Lalsawma, "The Work of the Holy Spirit and Tribal Religious Emotionalism" M.Th. Thesis Senate of Serampore College, 1968.

3 Lalsangkima Pachuau, "Thlarau lama intodelh nan," *Kristian Tlangau* LXXX / 959 (September, 1991), 20

II. Purpose of the Research

From the above elaboration of the problem, it is clear that the church is in confusion. At the same time, the church needs to revive and learn lessons from the occurrence. So, the purposes of this research are as follows:

1. To know the reasons why the main speaker K. Lalhmingliana of El-Bethel Team preaching's is popular, attractive and interesting.
2. To answer the following questions:
    - What are his favourite theological themes and Biblical texts?
    - What is the method and homiletic structure of his sermons?
    - What are the characteristic features of his preaching?
    - What is the theology of his preaching?
    - What are the main homiletic and theological problems in his preaching?
    - Does the preaching have a negative or positive impact on the life of the Church and the society in Mizoram?
3. To understand what the Church can learn from this research.
4. To suggest ways and means for the pastors and lay preachers of Church to improve their preaching.

III. Location of the Study

Both the Chanmari and Dawrpui Vengthar pastorates[4] are under Presbyterian Church of India, Mizoram Synod. Chanmari and Dawrpui Vengthar pastorates are situated in Aizawl city and they are among the first groups who invited the El-Bethel Team as pastorates in Aizawl city. They are one of the most affected and greatly influenced during the first part of El- Bethel revival movement in Mizoram.

1. Dawrpui Vengthar Pastorate: Vengthar Church which was later known as Dawrpui Vengthar church became, a full-fledged

---

4 Pastorate signifies the area looked after by one pastor, under the Presbyterian Church in Mizoram. One pastor one church is not possible till today, one pastor looks after many churches.

church on 2nd February 1958.[5] From this Dawrpui Vengthar church another three full-fledged churches have arisen. Chawnpui church in 1968,[6] Vaivakawn Church in 1971[7] and Dinthar church in 1977.[8]

The 1968 Synod Meeting[9] of the Mizoram Presbyterian Church resolved to create a new pastorate from the existing Dawrpui pastorate. The resolution was implemented and Vengthar became the station for the in-charge pastor. The first Vengthar pastorate meeting was held at Sairang Church on 6-8 March 1970.[10] There are nine churches under this new pastorate; they are Sairang, Sakawrtuichhun, Tanhril, Luangmual, Vengthar, Rangvamual, Tuikual, Chawnpui and Sihhmui churches.

The 1971 Synod Meeting resolved to create another pastorate from the existing Vengthar pastorate called Sairang Pastorate. There are seven churches under Sairang pastorate and there are five churches,[11] remain under the Vengthar pastorate. Later by the resolution of the 1984, Synod[12] Vengthar pastorate was divided again

---

5 "Kohhran Indan leh Rawngbawltu Nghet neih thu," *Dawrpui Vengthar Presbyterian Kohhran Chanchin 1955-2000: New Millennium Souvenir*, (Aizawl: Dawrpui Vengthar Kohhran, 2001), 13. Hereafter cited as *Dawrpui Vengthar Presbyterian Kohhran Chanchin 1955-2000: New Millennium Souvenir.*

6 "Dawrpui Vengthar Kohhran atanga Indangte," *Dawrpui Vengthar Presbyterian Kohhran Chanchin 1955-2000: New Millennium Souvenir ...*, 196.

7 Ibid.

8 Upa Ramhmangaiha Ralte, "Dinthar Kohhran Chanchin, (History of Dinthar church)" *Presbyterian Church of India: Dinthar: Aizawl Silver jubilee Souvenir (15.8. 1976-15 2001)* (Aizawl: Dinthar Presbyterian Kohhran, 2001), 13. *Dawrpui Vengthar Presbyterian Kohhran Chanchin 1955-2000: New Millennium Souvenir...*, 196.

9 Synod is constitutionally the top authority over each unit of the Presbyterian Church. Presbyterian Church of India has different units, each unit has different Synod, and the synod meeting is conducted annually and determines all the subjects related to the churches under its jurisdiction.

10 "Dawrpui Vengthar Pastor Bial Dinchhuah Dan Chanchin," *Dawrpui Vengthar Pastor Bial Silver Jubilee 1969-1994 Souvenir* (Aizawl: The Presbyterian Church of India Dawrpui Vengthar Pastor Bial, 1994), 4. Hereafter cited as *Dawrpui Vengthar Pastor Bial Silver Jubilee 1969-1994 Souvenir.*

11 Vengthar, Tuikual, Vaivakawn, Chawnpui and Luangmual.

12 "Dawrpui Vengthar Pastor Bial Dinchhuah Dan Chanchin," *Dawrpui Vengthar Pastor Bial Silver Jubilee 1969-1994 Souvenir ...*, 4.

and another pastorate called Luangmual pastorate was created. The seven churches[13] remained under the Vengthar pastorate. During this period there were 5638 full fledged church members in this pastorate.[14]

Again the 1992 Synod meeting resolved to create another new pastorate from Vengthar Pastorate called Vaivakawn Pastorate. From this period the name 'Dawrpui'[15] was added;[16] the following churches: Dawrpui Vengthar, Tuikual, Dinthar and Tuikual South remained under the Dawrpui Vengthar Pastorate and at present there were 3606 full communicant church members in this pastorate.[17]

Since the birth of this pastorate it gave birth to three new pastorates till today. This shows that this pastorate is a growing pastorate.

2. Chanmari Pastorate: The Presbyterian Church of India, Chanmari was opened on 17 July 1955[18] by Pastor Nikhama, and remained a Preaching Station up to 1957.[19] Chanmari Church

13 The seven churches are Vengthar, Tuikual, Vaivakawn, Dinthar, Hmunthar, Chawnpui and Zotlang Churches. "Dawrpui Vengthar Pastor Bial Dinchhuah Dan Chanchin," *Dawrpui Vengthar Pastor Bial Silver Jubilee 1969-1994 Souvenir ...*, 6.

14 "Synod Statistic," *1991 Synod Bu*, (Aizawl: Synod Literature and Publication Board, 1992), 326-327.

15 Dawrpui is the name of the Mother church of this Vengthar church, the location is also under the control of Dawrpui church, but due to the increase of church members, another church was established called Vengthar (new Locality) church.

16 "Dawrpui Vengthar Pastor Bial Dinchhuah Dan Chanchin," *Dawrpui Vengthar Pastor Bial Silver Jubilee 1969-1994 Souvenir ...*, 6.

17 "Synod Statistic,"*1993 Synod Bu*, (Aizawl: Synod Literature and Publication Board, 1994), 428-429.

18 "Chanmari Veng Presbyterian Kohhran," *Chanmari Kohhran leh Khawtlang Chanchin: Mizoram Gospel Centenary Souvenir 1994* (Aizawl: Chanmari Presbyterian Kohhran, 1993), 8. Hereafter cited as *Chanmari Kohhran leh Khawtlang Chanchin.*

19 "Chanmari Veng Presbyterian Kohhran," *Chanmari Kohhran leh Khawtlang Chanchin ...*, 8; "Chanmari Presbyterian Kohhran Chanchin Tlangpui," *Chanmari Presbyterian Kohhran Golden Jubilee 1955-2005 Souvenir* (Aizawl: Chanmari Presbyterian Church, 2005), 10. Hereafter cited as *Chanmari Presbyterian Kohhran Golden Jubilee 1955-2005 Souvenir.*

became a full-fledged church on 23.2.1958;[20] its mother church is Dawrpui Presbyterian Church. At the same time, the mother pastorate of this Chanmari Pastorate is Dawrpui Pastorate. Both Dawrpui Vengthar Pastorate and Chanmari Pastorate have the same mother church.

The 1974 Synod Meeting at Mission Veng resolved to create a new pastorate from the Dawrpui Pastorate and it was implemented on 5-7, March 1975, at Ramhlun South Church, Aizawl.[21] The new pastorate was then named Chanmari Pastorate and Chanmari became the station of the in-charge Pastor for the Pastorate. Pastor L. Z. Zolawma was the first in-charge pastor of this Pastorate.[22] There are six churches under the Chanmari Pastorate.[23]

After seven years, the 1980 Synod Meeting passed a resolution to create a new pastorate from the Chanmari Pastorate called Ramhlun Pastorate and it was implemented and the following three churches: Chanmari, Electric Veng, Ramthar Veng remained under the Chanmari pastorate.[24]

On 5th January 1986[25] a new full-fledged church was established from Chanmari PC called Chanmari West. The number of

---

20 Upa R. Lalhmangaiha, "Chanmari Presbyterian Kohhran Chanchin," *Mizoram Presbyterian Church Chanmari Pastor Bial Souvenir (1975-2000)*, (Aizawl: Chanmari Pastor Bial, 2000), 31. *Chanmari Kohhran leh Khawtlang Chanchin* ..., 8.

21 Upa L. Rozika, "Chanmari Pastor Bial Silver Jubilee (1975-2000)," *Mizoram Presbyterian Church Chanmari Pastor Bial Souvenir (1975-2000)*, (Aizawl: Chanmari Pastor Bial, 2000), 46. Hereafter cited as Upa L. Rozika, "Chanmari Pastor Bial Silver Jubilee (1975-2000)."

22 Upa J. H. Ramnghinglova, "Chanmari Pastor Bial Chanchin Tlangpui (1975-2000 AD)," *Mizoram Presbyterian Church Chanmari Pastor Bial Souvenir (1975-2000)*, (Aizawl: Chanmari Pastor Bial, 2000), 14.

23 Chanmari, Electric Veng, Ramhlun 'S', Ramhlun 'N', Ramhlun Vengthar and Electric Ramthar. Upa J. H. Ramnghinglova, "Chanmari Pastor Bial Chanchin Tlangpui (1975-2000 AD)," *Mizoram Presbyterian Church Chanmari Pastor Bial Souvenir (1975-2000)*, (Aizawl: Chanmari Pastor Bial, 2000), 12.

24 Upa L. Rozika, "Chanmari Pastor Bial Silver Jubilee (1975 -2000)" ..., 46.

25 Upa PC. Pakunga, "Chanmari West Presbyterian Kohhran Chanchin," *Mizoram Presbyterian Church Chanmari Pastor Bial Souvenir (1975-2000)*, (Aizawl: Chanmari Pastor Bial, 2000), 35.

churches became four under this pastorate and later on 4th February 1989 another new church was opened and inaugurated by Rev. Lalbiaktluanga, the Moderator of Aizawl Hmar Presbytery.[26] This new church was created by taking and combining 582 communicant members from the Electric Veng Church and Chanmari Church[27] and named Aizawl Venglai Church.[28] The number of the churches became five under this Chanmari pastorate till the year 1995, and there are 8036 communicant members in this pastorate. [29]

The 1996 Synod resolved to create another new pastorate from the Chanmari pastorate called Electric Veng Pastorate; [30] The following three churches: Chanmari, Chanmari West and Edenthar[31] remain under the Chanmari Pastorate and there were 4050 communicant members.[32]

Dawrpui Vengthar Pastorate is on the western side of Aizawl city and Chanmari Pastorate is on the eastern side of Aizawl city; they represent the east and western pastorates of Aizawl city.

These two neighbouring pastorates organized a joint camp program for the people of the two pastorates by inviting K. Lalhmingliana, El-Bethel Team speaker.

IV. Scope and Limitations of the Study

The study has been limited to two of the 160 Pastorates under the Presbyterian Church of Mizoram. The scope only covers Chanmari

---

26 *Presbyterian Kohhran Aizawl Venglai Kum 10 tlin lawmna Souvenir 1989-1999* (Aizawl: Presbyterian Church, Aizawl Venglai, 1999), 7.

27 *Presbyterian Kohhran Aizawl Venglai Kum 10 tlin lawmna Souvenir 1989-1999* ..., 10.

28 Upa L. Rozika, "Chanmari Pastor Bial Silver Jubilee (1975-2000)"..., 47.

29 *1995 Synod Bu*, (Aizawl: Synod Literature and Publication Board, 1996), 480-481.

30 Upa L. Rozika, "Chanmari Pastor Bial Silver Jubilee (1975-2000)"..., 47.

31 Previously Edenthar church was under the Chaltlang Pastorate, but the 1996 Synod resolved it to be under the pastorate of Chanmari. Since the beginning of 1997 they were under the pastorate of Chanmari. Upa B. Lalchhuangliana, "Edenthar Presbyterian Kohhran Chanchin," *Mizoram Presbyterian Church Chanmari Pastor Bial Souvenir (1975-2000)*, (Aizawl: Chanmari Pastor Bial, 2000), 37.

32 *1998 Synod Bu* (Aizawl: Synod Literature and Publication Board, 1999), 505.

Pastorate and Dawrpui Vengthar Pastorate of Mizoram Presbyterian Church within 1988-1997.

Since this El-Bethel Preaching ministry is a recent movement, it is difficult to get sufficient recorded material either in book form or on audio/ video cassettes. But some sermons are published in a book form.

V. Methodology

The research is mainly based on questionnaires, interview, library research and church documents.

1. Questionnaire

In this research, seventy questionnaire copies were distributed in the said two pastorates to the pastors, elders, lay leaders, *Kohhran Hmeichhe hruaitute* (Women front leaders in the church), KTP[33] *hruaitute* (Christian Youth Leaders), and lay people who witnessed their ministry and preaching. Out of seventy copies, fifty seven copies were returned to the researcher. Demographic detail is given in thc analysis of the Questionnaire in Chapter 6.

2. Interview

An interview was conducted with 40 persons, most of whom are from the two pastorates and a few from outside the pastorates because some have migrated outside of these two districts. Interviews were conducted in different open ended and unstructured type to the following different people groups:

Group No. 1 includes pastors and elders of the two pastorates.

Group No. 2 includes the lay people who witnessed and actively participated in the Camps of El-Bethel Team; organised by the Chanmari and Dawrpui Vengthar pastorates.

Group No. 3 includes the El-Bethel Team members and the relatives of K. Lalhmingliana who live in their home town called Champhai.[34]

---

33 KTP full form is Kristian Thalai Pawl which means Christian Youth Fellowship

34 This is the district capital of the Champhai district in the eastern side of Mizoram state; it is situated near the border of India and Myanmar. To have an interview in this town I spent three days since it is far from Aizawl city.

Each group answered separate questions in the interview since their involvement and participation in this gospel camp is different and the range of their knowledge and responsibility is different.

3. Method of Data Processing

In processing the data the following steps were taken to tabulate and analyse the data.

1. The answers to the open ended questions were classified according to their appropriate categories.
2. Tables were prepared to interpret the data.

4. Library Research

The El-Bethel Team organised a publication board called El-Bethel Publication Board, this board published journals called El-Bethel magazine since April 1990 and from this magazine most of the sermons and information were collected. It also published a collection of K. Lalhmingliana's sermons in a book called *El-Bethel Camp Sermon Vol-1* from which the sermons were analysed in this research work.

Aizawl Theological College also studied his ministries and their evaluation report and findings were helpful for this research.

Research also includes audio cassettes, video recordings of the preaching ministries of K. Lalhmingliana, and his personal biography which is unpublished, plus various other documents.

5. Hypothesis

The following hypotheses were formulated on the basis of general presuppositions:

1. The preaching of revival preacher is more attractive than that of the Pastors and elders of the conventional Church.
2. The El-Bethel sermons are not Biblically grounded.
3. There is no sufficient exposition of the texts in the camp preaching.
4. The El- Bethel evangelical preaching increased the collections of the Church offering.
5. The preaching created negative attitudes between the preaching of El- Bethel Team and the Elders and Pastors.

Chapter 2

The Formation of the El-Bethel Team and the Gospel Camp

I. Introduction

The following chapter is divided in to three main sections. Section 'I' takes up the life history of the main speaker of the El-Bethel team K. Lalhmingliana and the El-Bethel Revival Ministry. K. Lalhmingliana was a man of famous indegenous preacher, inspiring and main revival speaker as well as composer of native songs[35] in the El-Bethel Evangelical Team. He was 5' 6" tall with light curly hair, dark in colour, thick in stature and with a good physique.[36] Section 'II' takes up the organization of the Chanmari and Dawrpui Vengthar pastorates in relation to El-Bethel camp at Tanhril. Section 'III' takes up the relationship between Revival Department of Mizoram Presbyterian Church and El- Bethel Team.

35 He composed four songs in Mizo, 1. Bawlhlawh bawm (Dustbin), 2. Lal ngainatawm (Lovely Lord) 3. Chhiahhlawh College (the College of Servant), 4. Pumpelh phalloh intur No. (Unavoidable cup to drink). Thawmliani wife of K. Lalhmingliana interviewed on 19. 6. 2006, in their house at Champhai.

36 H. T. Kunga, "El-Bethel Camp Speaker Pu K. Lalhmingliana Hi tunge a nih?" *El-Bethel Magazine* 1/1 (April 1990): 4. (Here after cited as H. T. Kunga, "El-Bethel Camp"...).

1. The Biography of K. Lalhmingliana

1.1. Early Life: He was born on 21st December, 1937[37] in Sialsir Village of Mizoram to a Christian family. His father was Saikunga and his mother was Khuangzawni.[38] He passed Class I.[39] While he was a child his father Saikunga was an ecstatic and spiritual person.[40] He would dance in the worship service at Presbyterian Church in Sialsir village and the village chief accused him of being demon possessed. He was pulled and was knocked down in the church veranda.[41] Later he was sent to Aizawl for imprisonment. In the meantime, the father-in-law divorced his son-in-law.[42]

The family migrated to Chalrang village; there his mother re-married but unfortunately the new father died.[43] His elder sister also died at the age of 9. They became extremely poor; his real father also died in the village of Biate on 12th Dec. 1943.[44] Later his mother married again. His two brothers[45] joined Burmese Army.[46]

1.2. Life in Burma (Myanmar): He migrated to Burma in Jan.1954 and joined Evangelical Free Church of Burma (EFBC) and there he joined Burma Army.[47] In Sept.1958 he tried to join the US Army[48]

---

37 V. L Zaikima, *Ka Tla Fai Ta: Bethel Harhna leh a Behbawm, (Aizawl:* Lengchhawn Press, 1990), 64; H. T. Kunga, "El-Bethel Camp"... 4.

38 H. T. Kunga, "El-Bethel Camp"..., 4.

39 R. Vanlaltluanga, "Revival movement in Mizoram with Special Reference to Bethel Revival: A Theological Evaluation" (B.D Thesis, Senate of Serampore College, 1997), mentioned that he studied class II but after an interview and reading his own biography, it is confirmed that he was class I. *El-Bethel Team Speaker K. Lalhmingliana Chanchin (Autobiography of K. Lalhmingliana)* typed and edited on March 6-8, 2001 by Zohmangaiha of Chhinga Veng Aizawl: p. 3. Hereafter cited as *Autobiography of Lalhmingliana.*

40 *Autobiography of Lalhmingliana...*, 1.

41 Ibid.

42 Ibid.

43 Ibid., 2.

44 Ibid.

45 Hrangkhuma and Hrangchhinga. *Autobiography of Lalhmingliana* ..., 3.

46 *Autobiography of Lalhmingliana* ..., 3.

47 2nd Chin Rifles, R. Vanlaltluanga, "Revival Movements"..., 25.

48 R. Raltawna, "Nazaret Isua a kal ani," *Zo Ni Eng* 5/1 (January 17-24, 1990), 5.

to learn English.[49] For this he stole arms and ammunitions for the expense of his trip. But could not reach his destination and he lived among the Insurgency group for a year and returned to Pingkhung on Nov.1959.[50]

1.3. Family Life: On 1st April 1960 he married Vanmawii.[51] They had two children, but divorced in May 1963.[52] He then married Thawmliani on Sept.1963[53] and with her he had five sons and three daughters.

In 1973, he was elected as President of Bank Committee,[54] and also become the President of the Co-operative Society,[55] and ruled over 9 villages in their area.[56] People respected and admired him very much.[57] His status was good and he often helped others according to their needs.[58] He was active, intelligent, simple, hard working and good in administration.[59]

But life soon took a different turn. In 1975, he was charged and accused as an anti-Government activist on four grounds.[60] His

49 *Autobiography of Lalhmingliana...*, 5.

50 Ibid.

51 V. L. Zaikima, *Ka Tla Fai Ta: Bethel Harhna leh a Behbawm, (Aizawl*: Lengchhawn Press, 1990), 65.

52 R. Vanlaltluanga "Revival Movements"..., 26.

53 V. L. Zaikima, *Ka Tla Fai Ta...*, 65.

54 Ibid.

55 Ibid.

56 *Autobiography of Lalhmingliana...*, 5.

57 Ibid., 6.

58 V. L. Zaikima, *Ka Tla Fai Ta...*, 66.

59 *Autobiography of Lalhmingliana...*, 6.

60 1. An intelligence agent of the MNF (the freedom fighter for Mizoram). 2. Attempting the demolition of Run River Bridge between India and Burma. 3. To create Upper Chindwin as a Mizoram State.4. The leader in the Falam Bank robbery in 1968. *Autobiography of K. Lalhmingliana...*, 6; V.L Zaikima, *Ka Tla Fai Ta...*, 70; *Autobiography of Lalhmingliana...*, 7; Thawmliani w/o K. Lalhmingliana interview on 19. 6. 2006, in their house at Champhai says that, 'the reason of the charge was wrong and it was due to local politics.'

profession suddenly deteriorated. He was repeatedly spied[61] on by an intelligence agent from the Government of Burma. In 1979, he was offered the post of President by the Socialist Party in the Co-operative Society,[62] and he accepted.

One day Fertilizers[63] which were stored near his house were washed away due to heavy rain. He was charged to recover all the expenses since he was the President. For this he sold his land and belongings; from that day his financial condition deteriorated.[64] He stated, "My wife does not have spare dress, even my children did not have spare clothes, on Sunday the un-torn dress was worn in the forenoon by one boy and another brother wore the same dress in the afternoon."[65] They became extremely poor. He stated that:

> Once I was the helper of the poor but now God has put me in the status of the poor, helpless and needy, meanwhile intelligence office used to call me frequently to report myself, my wife and children were very much afraid during this time, because I might be executed any time. I am not afraid, if they put me in jail, it will be a chance of evangelism such was my conclusion, but it was not the thought of my wife and children. [66]

Time and again he was called to report himself to the authority which extremely agitated his family.[67]

1.4. Spiritual Life in Burma and the Call of God: In Feb.1962 he accepted Jesus Christ as his personal Saviour. He thought that the Holy Spirit was with him, according to Ephesians 1:13. During those days he stated that:

61 Thawmliani w/o K. Lalhmingliana interviewed on 19. 6. 2006, in their house at Champhai, Mizoram.

62 *Autobiography of Lalhmingliana…*, 13.

63 Ibid., 12.

64 Ibid., 13.

65 Ibid., 13-14.

66 Ibid., 18-22.

67 Khiangthuama, Ramdinzauva, Chanchinmawia, Laldinthari and Thawmliani w/o K. Lalhmingliana, interview on 19.6.2006, in their house at Champhai, Mizoram.

> I really hate the bad people, I used to strike the drunkards, they are afraid of me, and whenever they see me they used to run away from me, since I got the power and support from friends and Burma Government. They accept me as a good preacher; I received many greeting from people. I often preached that prayer for the fresh fellowship of the Holy Spirit is not needed; Holy Spirit was given in the day of Pentecost, and remained with us, such is my opinion.[68]

While he was at home alone on 18th April 1978 he received a fresh anointing of the Holy Spirit.[69] Using a portion of one song "*Thinlung tithianghlimtu, tlarau pianthartirtu*" (sanctifier of heart, inspirer of the rebirth of soul), unstoppable tears rolled down, and he realized that his previous ministry and services were useless and nothing. He was angry and felt it difficult to accept this new inspiration because he was already reborn in Feb.1964.[70] Then he went to the garden but the soft voice remained in his heart on the way. He stated "I cried, and said, 'take away the common knowledge of son-ship, because of this I could not know you; rather make me the smallest among the servants from now onward.'"[71] He said "I do not really know what I said, but later it reminded me that my way is the way of Servant hood. [72] He calls this incident as the 'Baptism of the Holy Spirit.'[73] After he received the baptism of the Holy Spirit on 18th April 1978[74] his whole life changed. He said, "I realized that the fresh fellowship of the Holy Spirit is really required in the Christian life."[75] One day, while he was preaching based on John 3:16-17, the Holy Spirit used

---

68 *Autobiography of Lalhmingliana ...*, 9.

69 R. Raltawna, "Nazareth Isua a kal ani," *Zo Ni Eng* 5/1 (January 17-24, 1990), 5.

70 *Autobiography of Lalhmingliana...*, 7; H. T. Kunga, "El-Bethel Camp Speaker Pu K. Lalhmingliana Hi tunge a nih? (Who is K. Lalhmingliana, Speaker of El-Bethel Team.)" *El-Bethel Magazine* 1/ 1(April, 1990), 4.

71 *Autobiography of Lalhmingliana...*, 8.

72 Ibid.

73 *El-Bethel Magazine* 1/1 (April, 1990), 4.

74 K. Lalhmingliana, *El-Bethel Camp Sermon* (Aizawl: El-Bethel Publication Board, 1993), 2.

75 *Autobiography of K. Lalhmingliana...*, 10.

John 5 of the encounter of Jesus and the paralyzed man who had been ill for 38 years. He said: I feel that I was also with them, when I heard that Jesus was asking, "Do you want to be made well?" If he say, "Yes, I want to be made well," there would be no effect upon me, but his answer was very shameful to me saying that, "Sir, I have no one to put me into the pool when the water is stirred up; and while I am making my way, someone else steps down ahead of me." When I heard his answer, I really feel pain that I am the one who did not help and avoid my duty, I was really surprised, humiliated and have nothing to say to God, I saw myself guilty. My heart was full of pain, and then I pray to God by telling my commitment that, "God, from now onward make me as a man of help for those who are helpless." From that day onwards my life was really changed and many helpless people are coming to my house and I help them as much as possible. This was my turning point toward God's ministry.[76]

From this time he was convinced by the word in Isaiah 53:6 "And the Lord has laid on Him the iniquity of us all." He realized and acknowledged that his way is the way of servant hood. The word "Servant" was really lovely and beautiful to him.[77]

1.5. Return to Mizoram: In Jan. 1987, he migrated to Zotlang and stayed for four months. There he sold his house for Rs. 5000.[78] On 24th May 1987 he crossed the border river of Mizoram called *Tiau Lui*,[79] and stayed at *Kelkang* village having only Rs. 225.00.[80] He presented himself for membership in the Kelkang Presbyterian Church but he was rejected due to the absence of Church Migration Certificate.[81]

---

76 *Aautobiography of K. Lalhmingliana...*, 10, K. Lalhmingliana, *El-Bethel Camp Sermon...*, 2-3.

77 *Autobiography of Lalhmingliana...*, 8.

78 *Autobiography of Lalhmingliana...*, 26.

79 Tiau Lui is the boundary river between India and Burma which is in the eastern part of Mizoram state.

80 *Autobiography of Lalhmingliana...*, 27- 28.

81 *Autobiography of Lalhmingliana...* 27. Church migration certificate is demanded to every migrated church member for further registration and for future ministry in the church which they are going to register themselves. This is the resolution and conventional practice of Presbyterian Church in Mizoram.

Later, he migrated to Champhai and he was officially registered by Zotlang Presbyterian Church.[82] According to H. T. Kunga, "God had shattered his land and house, and his main vocation. His comfort zone was shattered completely. Since then he was regularly inspired by the Holy Spirit."[83]

1.6. His Qualities in the Family: Beyond his organization in preaching ministry he was by nature humble, good tempered, patient and friendly. He was very hard working, ambitious and a man of self support and unflinching under suffering.[84] He was nationalist in mind,[85] and artist in drama show.[86] He taught all types of works to his children,[87] he never differentiate the work of boys and girls, women and men.[88] His children never ignored any type of work entrusted to them.[89] He was not highly educated but wise and good in administration.[90] He was not a disturbing person but was rather careful and behaved properly.[91] His voice was clear and good in articulation.

K. Hminga was a God-fearing man, a man of prayer and who used to pray together with his wife regularly.[92] He was regular in telling bed-time stories to his children. He was regular and serious in conducting family devotions just after every dinner. He taught

82 *Autobiography of Lalhmingliana...*, 30.

83 K. Lalhmingliana, *El-Bethel Camp Sermon...*, 2.

84 V. L. Zaikima, *Ka Tla Fai Ta...*, 65.

85 Ibid.

86 Ibid.

87 Khiangthuama s/o K. Lalhmingliana interviewed on 19.6.2006, in the house of his father at Champhai

88 Khiangthuama.

89 Ramdinzauva s/o K. Lalhmingliana interviewed on 19.6.2006, in the house of his father at Champhai, Mizoram.

90 Mr. Lal Thanchhunga interviewed on 28.4.2006 in his house, K. Hawla interviewed on 28.4.2006 in his house Tuikual, Aizawl, Mizoram.

91 Lianzuali w/o Rozinga interviewed on 12.5.2006 in their house at Chanmari, their house is the dwelling place of K. Lalhmingliana while he was in Chanmari, Mizoram.

92 Thawmliani w/o K. Lalhmingliana interviewed on 19.6.2006, in their house at Champhai, Mizoram.

his children frequently to put their trust in the Lord,[93] and they were active supporters of their father's ministry. His son Madina was good in singing and he used to sing in his father's ministry.[94] But his sons were not free from all social evils; one of his children was an alcoholic, and K. Hminga was also a heavy smoker.[95]

1.7 Miracle: Rev Sangbera, pastor in-charge of their local church, had interviewed him on 16th March 2004[96] while he was sick. There he shared his favourite texts, Colossians 2: 6 and Jeremiah 17: 8. Many healing took place in his ministry,[97] among which; the greatest event in his ministry to him was the preaching ministry in Nagaland, when a blind Hindu *sadhu* (priest) came to him and recovered sight then converted into Christianity; that was unforgettable to him."[98]

1.8. The Health Problems and Death of the Famous Speaker: After having El-Bethel Camp from 22-27th Jan. 1990 at Tanhril, it was discovered that he was suffering from high blood pressure and diabetes,[99] but he continued his preaching ministry for more than ten years.[100] Later, he had cancer and suffered for a long period. He delivered his last two sermons on 21st March 2004 at Champhai Vengthlang; the theme was 'New Jerusalem,' based on Revelation

93 Chanchinmawia s/o K. Lalhmingliana interviewed on 19.6.2006, in the house of his father at Champhai, Mizoram.

94 H. T. Kunga, "El-Bethel Camp Speaker Pu K. Lalhmingliana Hi tunge a nih?"..., 4.

95 Thawmliani. Smoking and Mizo culture is closely related, since it was practised from the forefather, smoking is not regard as sin among the Mizos.

96 *Funeral VIDEO C.D., of K. Lalhmingliana, Speaker of El-Bethel Team, 20th May 2004.*

97 34 people are healed in the Biate El-Bethel camp, "Biate a El-Bethel team rawngbawlnaa damna changte *El-Bethel Magazine* 3/5, (July, 1992): 19-20; 13 people are healed in East Lungdar camp, "Bethel Report East Lungdar," *El-Bethel Magazine* 3/3, (September, 1992): 17-18; 406 people are healed in Songpijang, "Bethel Report: Songpijang leh Changpijang," *El-Bethel Magazine* VII/3, (July, 1995), 12-14.

98 Ibid.

99 V. L. Zaikima, *Ka Tla Fai Ta...*, 85.

100 Some times he could not preach due to illness, *El-Bethel Magazine* 2/15, (July, 1991), 15.

21:18-21. Two months after delivering the sermon on 'New Jerusalem' he left the world to enter the New Jerusalem on 20th May, 2004.[101]

2. Origin and Development of the Ministry

2.1. Ministry in Burma: In Burma during 1979-1982 K. Lalhmingliana used to preach the gospel to the Burmese and often spent the night with them. Nine Burmese were converted to Christianity.[102] From Sept.1983 he began to work with C. Lalchungnunga.

C. Lalchungnunga was an evangelist and was born on 10 Feb. 1942.[103] In 1981, he received the revelation of God related to the love of God. Because of this he called himself as Agape Gospel Puangtu (AGP).[104] He started his ministry among the drug addicts and alcoholics in Burma. He organised crusades, camps and campaigns in different villages.[105] In each village often he selected a secluded area in the outskirt (for having prayer and meditation) which he called 'Bethel.' He invited the campers to join him in his Bethel. That was the beginning of the Bethel Movement.[106] In the *Mamoh* Camp in 1982 he took all the campers to his Bethel place to offer prayer, and found it very effective.[107] Henceforth, it became regular practice to bring all the campers to the Bethel. In 1983, he formed an evangelistic team called Agape Gospel Puangtu (Herald); the Chief

---

101 *Funeral VIDEO C.D., of K. Lalhmingliana, Speaker of El-Bethel Team, 20th. May 2004.*

102 *Autobiography of Lalhmingliana…*, 14; V. L. Zaikima, *Ka Tla Fai Ta…*, 69.

103 V. L. Zaikima, *Ka Tla Fai Ta…*, 56. In the B.D thesis of R. Vanlaltluanga date of birth is recorded as 10th February 1940. Thesis…, 25.

104 V. L. Zaikima, *Ka Tla Fai Ta…*, 57.

105 In Burma, he organised 24 crusades and ten gospel camp. V. L. Zaikima, *Ka Tla Fai Ta…*, 58.

106 V. L. Zaikima, *Ka Tla Fai Ta…*, 57.

107 Ibid., 59.

Assistant was K. Lalhmingliana. Their team also worked together along with evangelist Rohmingliana[108] for a short while.[109]

The main aim of their team was to bring back alcoholics, drug abusers and commercial sex workers (CSWs) toward the normal life. For this they built a Rescue Centre for 20 and inaugurated it on 4th May 1984. It was successful and effective but due to lack of financial support it was stopped in 1986.[110] Both of them migrated to Mizoram separately and later settled in Champhai.

2.2. Ministry in Mizoram: After migration to Mizoram the first camp was organized by Zotlang PC in July 1987 for alcoholics and drug abusers. They invited C. Lalchungnunga as speaker. It was successful and many campers received new life and received a fresh anointing of the Holy Spirit. There K. Hminga joined the team again as a counsellor. He was the main in-charge of Bethel Prayer and formation of Rendezvous (RV) in the Team. Before they entered the central part of Mizoram they had gospel camp in the Presbyterian Churches of the eastern part of Mizoram.[111]

2.3. The Birth of El-Bethel Team: While working together with C. Lalchungnunga on 10th Oct.1987, K. Hminga[112] received call through Psalm 92:10.[113] K. Hminga thought that it was a theme for his sermon. But later, he realized that it was the call for his future ministry. The AGP visited several villages, and wherever they went,

108 Evangelist Rohmingliana belonged to Methodist Church, in Burma (Myanmar), later come to Mizoram and established an evangelistic team called Truth Mission Evangelical Fellowship (TMEF).

109 Interview with Evangelist Rohmingliana on 27.4.2006 at Aizawl. And also Thawmliani w/o K. Lalhmingliana interviewed on 19.6.2006, in their house at Champhai.

110 V. L. Zaikima, *Ka Tla Fai Ta…*, 70.

111 Like Champhai, Ruantlang, Kahrawt, Khawzawl, Khawbung, Khawzawl Venglai, Sialhawk, Biate, Kawlkulh, Khuangleng. C. Vanlallawma, *Bethel Revival leh Lausanne Thuthlung* (Aizawl: Lengchhawn Press, 1990), 4.

112 From now onwards instead of using the full form K. Lalhmingliana, K. Hminga will be used.

113 "But you have exalted my horn like that of the wild ox; you have poured over me fresh oil." (NRSV).

the flame of revival was growing enormously.[114] They decided to create another new team from the existing team.[115] After this on Feb.1988, they were separated[116] and K. Hminga formed a separate team.

Lalchungnunga retained the name 'AGP' for his Team. Most senior members remained with Lalchungnunga,[117] and K. Hminga was followed by 97[118] young and newborn drug addicts and alcoholics[119] and they moved towards N. Khawbung[120] and other villages[121] to organize the first gospel camp. This was the beginning of his team.

Firstly, they were known as Mr. Hminga's Team.[122] But in 1988, God gave them a name, the "*El-Bethel Evangelical Team*,"[123] after his prayer to give the name on 29th June 1988 in Vanzau village.[124] His

114 "El-Bethel Camp Mualpui leh Chite ami Zawhfel anileh ta," *Forum* 1/4 (February 20-27, 1990), 5.

115 V. L. Zaikima, *Ka Tla Fai Ta…*, 60.

116 There were reasons for their separation, K. Hminga wanted to nurture the drug addicts who were born again through their ministry, but Lalchungnunga was reluctant to do so because he was afraid that the church might be displeased with those 'sinners.' R. Vanlaltluanga…., 26. K. Hminga wanted to organize separate camp from general camp for the ministers, but Lalchungnunga did not take much effort for that. There was less chance to preach for K. Hminga in the Team. Thawmliani interviewed on 19.6.2006. So he wanted to have a separate team for more time to preach, since he convinced himself that he was called out and anointed by God. V.L Zaikima, *Ka Tla Fai Ta…*, 71.

117 Upa R. Lallianzuala interviewed on 29.4.2006

118 V. L. Zaikima, *Ka Tla Fai Ta…*, 71.

119 Thawmliani w/o K. Lalhmingliana interviewed on 19.6.2006, in their house at Champhai.

120 Upa R. Lallianzuala of Chanmari, interviewed on 29.4.2006.

121 Then camp in Sesih, Leisenzo, Bulfek, Salvation Army of Kahrawt Veng, Champhai Zotlang, Kelkang, Buang and Bungzung follows. V. L. Zaikima, *Ka Tla Fai Ta…*, 72.

122 V. L. Zaikima, *Ka Tla Fai Ta…*, 72. H. T. Kunga…, 5.

123 Lalhmangaiha, "A Study of the Theology of Three Mizo Itinerant Evangelists in the Light of Pauline kerugma: an Evaluation" (B.D. Thesis, Senate of Serampore College, 1997).

124 K. Hawla Sailo, "El Bethel Harhna (Tran. Revival)," *Harhna: Mizoram Revival Centenary Souvenir (1906-2006)* (Aizawl: Synod Revival Committee,

understanding of the name of the team was related with Genesis 28: 19 that it was door of heaven opened and called Beth'el: but when Jacob returned, he was called by God to go to Beth'el (Gen. 35: 1), and due to this second visit he called El-Beht'el not Beth'el (Gen.35:7). To him the difference of the way to Beth'el and the way to El-Beth'el was really different and meaningful;[125] the way how it was approached was without preparation in the first time, but the second time it was with full of preparation by purifying and changing clothes.[126] So he accepted that El-Bethel is the gift of God for the name of his team.[127]

After six months of having the name of the team in Dec.1988 he entered Aizawl, and camp[128] was organized by P. C. Bawngkawn[129] with his team. While he was inside the city bus one lady asked the motto of his team; he answered "*reaching the un-reached to whom the ministry of other evangelists (independent preachers) and the ministry of the church never reaches and to evangelize drug addicts, alcoholics and commercial sex workers.*"[130] The lady replied, "Your motto seems to be the gospel that reaches sinners."[131] That attached in the mind of K. Hminga and it was accepted for the motto of the team. Before, temporarily they called "Humility" as their motto, then "*Humility-The Gospel that Reaches Sinners*" was recognized and accepted as the motto of the Team.

2.4. Administrative setup of El-Bethel Team: When the El-Bethel Evangelical Team was formed, proper administration and function was very much needed since the members of the team were from different areas and backgrounds. In the beginning there were: Director, Speaker, Chairman, Secretary and Treasurer, in the Team;

2006), 546.

125 *Autobiography of Lalhmingliana*..., 31.

126 *Autobiography of Lalhmingliana*..., 31.

127 Ibid.

128 The settings, forms, nature, items, routine, etc. will be discussed in this Chapter II, C.

129 *Autobiography of Lalhmingliana*..., 31.

130 Ibid.

131 Ibid., 32.

but they could not go any further.[132] Later it was changed to the following designation:[133]

Speaker :	K. Lalhmingliana
Deputy Speaker :	K. Vanlalngena
Secretary :	M.C. Lalfala[134]
Counsellors:	1. R. Biakhmingthanga, 2. Hauthuama, 3. L. Sangzuala, 4. Lalduhpuia, 5. K. Malsawma, 6. Malsawmdawngliana, 7. Hmangaihzuala

Conveners of Tawngtai Khawl (Prayer Machine): There were three conveners in this department: 1. C. Lalhmingliana, 2. C. Khualdawla and 3. D. Thangliana.

Members of Prayer machine *(Tawngtai Khawl)*: There are sixty four (64) members[135] in this *Prayer Machine* group. The number of members is not fixed, it always changed. They are the regular volunteers; their main duty was regular (unceasing) prayer for the team and the campers. At times they also give advice to the team, as well as to the campers and also taught the Word of God.[136]

2.5. New Team: In Oct.1991 the deputy speaker of El-Bethel Team, Mr. Vanlalngena created a separate team and he became an independent preacher. He was working as the house father of Jeriko Khualbuk (Inn of Jericho). The other two Counsellors Mr. Lalsangzuala and K. Lalthlengliana also became independent and introduced a separate Team[137] from the mother El-Bethel Team; both of them received Rs.1000 each from the mother team for the

132 V. L. Zaikima, *Ka Tla Fai Ta…*, 73.

133 Ibid; the post of Secretary was not mentioned in "El-Bethel Evangelical Team Lo Indin dan," *El-Bethel Magazine* 1/1 (April 1990): 5. The name of the Secretary was not known during this time.

134 He was reborn in the camp at Darlung on 30th October to 4th November 1989.

135 "El-Bethel Evangelical Team lo indin dan (Origin and Development of El-bethel Team)," *El-Bethel Magazine* 1/1 (April, 1990), 5.

136 C. Vanlallawma, *Bethel Revival leh Lausanne Thuthlung* (Aizawl: Lengchhawn Press, 1990), 8.

137 "El-Bethel Evangelical Team atanga Iptepui bat hrang, (Independent from El-bethel Team)" *El-Bethel Magazine* 2/16 (August, 1991), 10-11.

capital of their establishment.[138] A farewell meeting was organized on 4th July 1991 in the residence of Upa. Lalthianga Luangmual. The members became 31 in the existing El-Bethel Team.[139]

3. The Scope of El-Bethel Team and Their Ministry

In the Bethel revival movement, preaching plays an important role, but in the other revival movement in Mizoram; preaching is not regarded as the leading role and main cause.[140] The first revival of Mizoram in 1906[141] preaching did not play much important role. The main theme of the revival was '*awareness of sins and confessions.*'[142] The theme of the 1913[143] revival movement[144] was *the second coming of Jesus Christ.*[145] In 1919 revival movement the main interest was *the cross of suffering, the suffering of Christ;* in 1934 the revival movement turns towards the theme of *The Holy Spirit and the gifts of the Holy Spirit.*[146] In all these revivals, preaching was not the main events, and no particular distinguished preacher was mentioned including 1984 revival. But in El-Bethel revival movement preaching was the main event, this is the distinction of El-Bethel revival from the rest of other revivals in Mizoram.

The main focus of the team was reaching the 'un-reached'[147] people through their preaching ministry. There are no socio, economic, political and geographical boundaries. The Team moved

---

138 "El-Bethel Evangelical Team Lo Indin dan, (Origin and Development of El-bethel Team)," *El-Bethel Magazine* 1/1 (April 1990), 5.

139 "El-Bethel Evangelical Team atanga Iptepui bat hrang," *El-Bethel Magazine* 2/16 (August, 1991), 10-11.

140 Rev. Lalsawma, *Revivals the Mizo Way,* (Aizawl: Lalsawma, Mission Vengthlang, 1994), 170.

141 Rev. H. Remthanga & Rev Lalbiaktluanga, *Kohhran Chanchin (1500-1990),* (Aizawl: Synod Publication Board, 1990), 249.

142 C. Vanlallawma, *Bethel Revival...,* 19.

143 C. B. Firth, *An Introduction to Indian Church History* (Delhi: ISPCK, 2001), 270.

144 Rev. H. Remthanga, *Kohhran Chanchin...,* 249.

145 C. Vanlallawma, *Bethel Revival...,* 19. Rev. H. Remthanga, *Kohhran Chanchin...,* 249.

146 C. Vanlallawma, *Bethel Revival ...,* 19.

147 The people who are not reached by the general ministry of the churches.

to where they are invited either by the church or Joint Committee of the local churches of various denominations.

3.1. Ministry to Commercial Sex Workers, Alcoholics and Drug Addicts: From the beginning the main concern of K. Hminga was reaching the un-reached who were neglected by the society and church's ministry. He used to invite them and approached them and tried to communicate with them.[148]

On 15th May 1989 he organized a home crusade for the drug addicts and alcoholics in the house of Vanlalngena, Electric Veng;[149] five of them recovered. Then he approached Commercial Sex Workers (CSW) in the hotel called Hotel Florida;[150] they were ten in number,[151] but he was not accepted and they ran away after his prayer.[152] On 8th December, 1989 (by night), he dressed like a street boy and he visited a Bar (*Tuitling Bar*).[153] There he met seven CSWs; he drove them to an isolated place with wine.[154] Later, he prayed for them, and when he was identified the girls became very angry charged that he was cheating them.[155] On 10th December, 1989 he went to the same Bar; and there he met Lalhriatpuii a famous CSW.[156] He invited her with her friends[157] to come to the Camp. Later, they

148 While Gospel camp was in Bawngkawn church, one lady proudly said to him, "our locality is the main centre of commercial sex workers, and there were 120 houses who were local illicit liquor sellers, but they were driven away by the combined acts of the church and the society; only 20 families of illicit liquor sellers are stayed behind at present." He was very disappointed and tears rolled down, then he stated that '*they are the sisters of our Lord,*' and he asked her where they would be now and how can he find such people and bring them to the Lord? Such was his compassion towards these people. *Autobiography of K. Lalhmingliana...*, 31.

149 He was the Deputy Speaker of Legislative Assembly, Mizoram.

150 *Autobiography of Lalhmingliana...*, 36.

151 V. L. Zaikima, *Ka Tla Fai Ta...*, 74. *Autobiography of Lalhmingliana...*, 37.

152 *Autobiography of Lalhmingliana...*, 37.

153 Name of a Bar, where commercial sex workers are easily available, V. L. Zaikima, *Ka Tla Fai Ta...*, 83.

154 K. Hawla Sailo, "El-Bethel Harhna" ..., 545.

155 V. L. Zaikima, *Ka Tla Fai Ta...*, 83.

156 Ibid.

157 Mabiaki and Hlimpuii.

came to the camp on 28th December, 1989.[158] They repented and were reborn. [159] She became the source to identify their centre[160] and her friends many CSWs were invited; 15 of them were collected and they were brought to the camp during 22nd-27th January, 1990.[161] Many CSWs and alcoholics and drug addicts were brought to Christ through this outreach ministry.

3.2. Ministry to the Poor: Since June 1978 he could not eat food without the presence of the poor.[162] He thought of himself as being far worse than a rich man in the story of *the Rich Man and Lazarus* (Luke 16: 19-31). Whenever they were invited to have Gospel Camp from various churches their team first approached mostly the poor people and stayed in their home and remained till the camp is over.[163] The poor people did not have time for camp; they needed to work every day to earn their livelihood. So, remembering their problems some of the Team members were appointed to work for them and took their place in their daily works.[164] The poor people were sent to the camp,[165] to receive and listen to the Word of God.

3.3. Ministry to Central Jail: During 17-23rd April, 1990, the Deputy Speaker Vanlalngena and some of the team members organized El-Bethel camp in Central Jail.[166] 430 prisoners attended this camp and it was very successful.[167]

---

158 Lalhriatpuii, *Ka Damna Isua* (Aizawl: Bawlliana Mission Veng. 2004), 59.

159 Ibid., 64, 65; V.L Zaikima, *Ka Tla Fai Ta…,* 84.

160 V. L. Zaikima, *Ka Tla Fai Ta…,* 84.

161 Ibid., 85.

162 Ibid., 69.

163 V. L. Zaikima, *Ka Tla Fai Ta…,* 74; *Autobiography of Lalhmingliana…*, 71.

164 V. L. Zaikima, *Ka Tla Fai Ta…,* 74; *Autobiography of Lalhmingliana…*, 71.

165 Chanchinmawia s/o K. Lalhmingliana interviewed on 19. 6. 2006, in the house of his father at Champhai.

166 C. Lalhmangaiha, "El-Bethel at Central Jail," *El-Bethel Magazine* 1/1 (April, 1990), 2.

167 *El-Bethel Magazine* 1/2 (May, 1990), 14.

3.4. Ministry to All: In this El-Bethel revival movement all types of people were covered: Pastors, elders, evangelist, politicians,[168] magistrates,[169] officers, business people, CSWs,[170] the poor and the rich, sweepers, drug abusers, alcoholics, makers of illicit liquor and sellers, and there was no discrimination in sex, and no age bar. However, special camp was organized for children separately.

4. The Nature and Functions of 'The Camp of El-Bethel Team'

Usually El-Bethel Camp commenced on Tuesday and concluded on Saturday, taking five days. Before camp started, necessary information was given to the people regarding the place, date and time, and things to bring and not to bring and to approach the camp with their own expenses.

4.1. The Two Categories of El-Bethel Camp: Camp was organized two times, for two types of groups.

4.1.1. Ministers Camp (Rawngbawltu Camp): This first camp was for the ministers, Here 'ministers' does not mean only ordained persons but even those who have responsibilities and particular appointment in various church activities. This included pastors, elders, Sunday school teachers, preachers, Wednesday Night Theme study leader, Worship Opener (doing Bible reading and prayers), Song Leaders, Offering Collectors, Various Committee Members, Women Committee Member, and Youth Committee Members.

4.1.2. General Camp: This camp was for all types of people**.** It was for the members of the organizing churches, members of other denominations, Christians and non-Christians. Special preference was given to the church members of the organizer due to the limitation of seats and accommodation. But some people entered the camp without having tickets.

---

168 "Bethel Camp thlipui in a nuai," *Sakeibaknei* 1/283 (February 16, 1990), 10; "El-Bethel Camp Mualpui leh Chite ami Zawhfel anileh ta." *Forum* 1/4 (February 20-27, 1990), 5.

169 R. C. Thanga, "El-Bethel ah ka kal ve," *Sakeibaknei* 4 /707 (November, 1990), 4-5.

170 *Harhna* Daily news paper Vol. XVI (February, 1990), 1.

4.2. The Camp Procedure: In organizing Camp, the responsibilities were divided between the organiser, and the El-Bethel team.

4.2.1. The Responsibility of the Organiser

The Place: The place is selected by the organizing churches according to their convenience. Each camper came at their own expenses.

Ticket System: The organizing committee arranged tickets for the campers; it was only Rs.10. Later, Rs 30 was fixed for each camper[171] since there are some people, who did not bring even rice for their food. On reaching the camp, the ticket (which was really difficult to get)[172] needed to be shown to the security, not for raising fund but to know the amount of food to make, to know the numbers of the campers and for accommodation.

Security and Medical: There were around 60 Security members and it was needed in every El-Bethel camp because the atmosphere was too hostile.[173] At the entrance of the camp area, checking tickets and the property of the campers was a very heavy responsibility. Many people flocked together and try to enter in the camp without ticket even from outside the organiser's area. In case of emergency medical department were in action. Drug addicts, alcoholics and some other ill health campers always needed treatment.[174]

Requirement for the Campers: Every camper was requested to carry the bedding, three kilograms of rice, rice plate, mug, Bible, song book, note book and personal necessities e.g. toiletries.[175]

Food and Lodging: Food and tea was served. Regarding lodging, separate accommodation for male and female was provided. There was a separate place for team members and the speaker was given a

---

171 *Harhna* XVI/ 43 (February, 1990), 1.

172 Rev. Robawiha, "Bethel – ah ka kal ve a," *Kristian Tlangau* LXXIX/ 950 (May, 1990), 11.

173 Some campers were drug addicts, alcoholics, politicians, lawyers, rich and poor, religious and irreligious; all types of people gathered there.

174 Dr. Zokhuma interviewed on 17.5.2006 at his residence.

175 Upa. Lalhluna, Secretary of the Organizing Committee letter to the author, 21st May 2006; Pi. Chuhveli interviewed on 12. 5. 2006; Upa V. L. Ruata interviewed on 29th. 4. 2006.

separate chamber. For Public health and sanitation proper number of toilets constructed and adequate supply of electricity and water was responsibility of the organizers before camp began.

Hall (Pandal): In El-Bethel Camp, Hall was the main centre for preaching, Bible study, and worship and singing. The organiser churches used to construct the pandal where they wanted to have El-Bethel camp. This construction was mainly done through voluntary social work by many people.

4.2.2. The Responsibility of the El-Bethel Team

The speaker and the team members were the authorities in this regard.

Preaching: This is the main event in the camp, usually 13 sermons are preached in a single Camp. ***Counselling Class:*** Mass counselling is conducted in the hall. Eight times counselling classes are held in a single Camp. ***Timetable*:** In every Camp same timetable prepared by the El-Bethel team was followed.

4.2.3. The Bethel Prayer: Introduction of Bethel Prayer is one of their contributions among the Mizo Christians. The word 'Bethel' means to the Team 'serious individual prayer in an isolated place.' The area for Bethel prayer was around 4 Sq. Kilometres in Tanhril area.[176] On the third and fourth day of the camp 11:30AM-1:00 PM, was for Bethel prayer. The Team divided all the campers into different groups under the leadership of the Team members; each group had 40-60 campers.[177]

The allotted area for male and female was different.[178] Before they go, each group was informed a particular place called R.V. (Rendezvous), to which all the group members were supposed to return after prayer. In this RV the group leaders were sitting together and pray for their respective group members. Each leader taught the prayer slogan and other important information.[179] The leaders

176 K. Hawla Sailo interviewed at his house.

177 K. Hawla Sailo, "El- Bethel Harhna" ..., 548.

178 Lal Thanchhunga, "El-Bethel leh Kei"... 5. (Unpublished article).

179 K. Hawla Sailo, "El- Bethel Harhna"..., 548. The campers were told that the areas had been dedicated to God by prayer and that no harm will come to

were usually young and some did not have proper education. Some officers, pastors and elders at first feel it very difficult to obey them.[180]

After receiving instructions each person went to different direction to places in which no one disturb another. There they prayed, confessed their sins and asked the forgiveness of God in a loud voice. The position may be according to their conveniences.[181] They ignored other voices or sounds. They are to ponder on prayer and opened themselves to hear the Lord.[182] They did not leave the place until some verse from the Bible or hymns impress them as the voice from the Lord. These words were recognized as coming from God because they come repeatedly to the mind or touch their heart. This prayer was mainly for 1 1/2 hours. After they received the answers of their prayer and a fellowship of the Holy Spirit they are overjoyed and returned to the R.V. There they put a small stick to mark that they have come back[183] and give the report of their testimony to the RV. This testimony is a mark of success in Bethel prayer. Some returned empty handed, or received nothing, so they needed to go again and again.

4.2.4. The Role of Singing in the Camp: One hour was given for singing between 2-3 PM on the first day. There was no time for singing on the second day. More time for singing was given on the third day 5:30-8:00 PM, 9:00-11:00PM; on Fourth day 7:00-9:00AM, 3-4

---

them, even from snakes or harmful insects, because the Holy Spirit covers the camp area. One report goes like this: "Those who went to have bethel-prayer found a snake and some actually prayed with a snake nearby, but these snakes crawled away from the campers. There has been a tremendous power of God that can be seen by the people; the atmospheres of the Serchhip town and its surrounding have been greatly changed" quoted from Lalhmangaiha... 34. *El-Bethel Magazine* 1/4 (July, 1990), 13.

180 Lalhmangaiha, "A Study of the Theology of Three Mizo Itinerant Evangelists in the Light of Pauline Kerugma: an Evaluation" (B.D. Thesis Senate of Serampore College, 1997).

181 Position may be standing, sitting, kneeling, laying, raising arm, rolling on the ground etc, and depending upon the personal interest of his/her prayer.

182 Lalhmangaiha, "A Study" ..., 34.

183 By counting the number of the sticks, the leaders can identify the numbers of the members who are not yet returned from his team. This was introduced first at Farkawn camp, on January, 1989. V. L. Zaikima, *Ka Tla Fai Ta...*, 73.

PM, 6:30-9:00, 10 PM-Onwards the last night was mainly singing and dancing throughout the night.[184] Overall, there was more than 14 hours for singing. Most of the songs were sung in traditional (indigenous) tunes. While singing most of the campers were dancing in praise of God. Dancing was regarded as the symbol of rejoicing due to the fresh inspiration of the Holy Spirit, victory over evil and surrender to God and witnessing of the Holy Spirit.

4.2.5. The Seeds of Faith: The word 'Seed Faith,' is used by Oral Robert, but it is more clear to me using 'the Seeds of Faith' and it make sense to me. This system was started first by the El-Bethel Team in Mizoram. One big container was set near the Information Office. The box was opened four to five times by those in-charges in a day. The campers used to drop their precious belongings,[185] money, jackets, shawls, blankets, gold chains, gold rings, sweaters, coats, watches, shoes. Some dropped the names of their belongings like cow, jeep, scooter, pig, etc.[186] People were free to drop any thing, but there was no compulsion. The materials were collected and disposed of by auction. The money was used for the expense in the camp and for helping the El- Bethel Team. Responsibility was taken by the organizing committee. Its theology will be discussed in another chapter.

4.2.6. Tawngtai Khawl (lit. Prayer Machine): Tawngtai Khawl was introduced by this Team. Membership register was maintained and the members were those who experienced the fellowship of the Holy Spirit through Camp. There was no age bar; both male and female, no discrimination in church denomination. There were 54 members[187] in this Tawngtai Khawl during 17-24 Jan. 1990.

Their activity was offering regular prayer for the Speaker, the Team and for all the Campers. They observed fasting and prayer.[188]

184 K. Hawla Sailo, "El- Bethel Harhna"..., 548.

185 "Mualpui El-Bethel Camp zawh ani," *Forum* 1/8 (April, 1990): 2; "El-Bethel Speaker Central Jail lamah alut ve ta,"*Forum* 1/12 (April, 1990): 5.

186 "Lawngtlai El-Bethel ah Sakei leh Sakhi an tel ve tlat," *Forum* 1/23 (July 4-9, 1990): 2.

187 R. Raltawna, "Nazaret Isua a kal ani,"*Zo Ni Eng* (January 17-24, 1990): 6.

188 Ibid.

They were the leaders of each group, and teachers of prayer slogan at the Bethel prayer. After their respective group members left to the forest, they come together in a place called RV, and pray for 2-4 hours. They were mainly 30-70 members. The size of the Tawngtai Khawl was not constant. Whoever returned from forest must report to this Tawngtai Khawl. As soon as they arrived, they were asked to share their testimonies,[189] and they offered thanksgiving prayer and they also prayed for them. If some camper could not give convincing or clear-cut testimony, they were sent back to the forest to offer more prayers.

This meant that their testimony must be acceptable to the Tawngtai Khawl. After sharing their testimonies they were sent to the Worship hall where singing was conducted. As they were called Tawngtai Khawl, offering prayer was their main responsibility for the inspirations of the Holy Spirit, for the success and good result of the Camp.

4.2.7. The Victory Procession: This was the last item in the camp just after morning meal. The Victory procession followed. To the team, Victory Procession was a must and this signified the victory over evil and proclamation of their new life in Christ. In the procession, campers raised both their arms and shouted in praise of Jesus.[190] And it was concluded by mass thanksgiving prayer. They departed the camp with having a new life and joyful heart with more desire to witness for Christ. Church members welcomed them; a wonderful meeting was there with tears of joy, and new experiences requesting the forgiveness from the depth of their heart from one another. That was a wonderful moment.[191]

5. Result of the El-Bethel Camp

Wherever camp was organized there was no discrimination in the denominational level, and there were no ethnic boundaries. His sermons were translated in to local languages where needed. The

189 Lal Thanchhunga, "El-Bethel leh Kei (My self and El-Bethel)" ..., 7. (Unpublished article)

190 C. Vanlallawma, *Bethel Revival* ..., 10.

191 K. Hawla Sailo, "El- Bethel Harhna"..., 548.

ministry of El-Bethel Team covered most of the states of North East India - Mizoram, Manipur,[192] Assam,[193] Meghalaya,[194] Tripura and Nagaland.[195] The secretary of Laisong El-Bethel Camp mentioned:

> We praise God for successful completion of the 1st and 2nd camp here at Laisong. We feel proud and consider ourselves lucky enough to be co-worker amongst you through this wonderful occasion. We have seen so many people coming from 36 villages to this camp to quench their spiritual thirst and witness God's miracle in the healing of disease suffered by people for many days. It is worth mentioning that God of mercy really works in us resulting in spiritual renewal in the life of his people.[196]

This shows that the ministry covered healing from sickness and revival in the churches throughout the North Eastern states among all types of people. As there was no discrimination[197] in the El-Bethel camp between male and female, big and small, old and young, rich and poor, they slept together, ate, prayed, sang, danced, and

---

192 R. Biakhmingthanga, "Manipur Rama El-Bethel Rawngbawlna Kalzel," *El-Bethel Magazine* 5/48, (April, 1994): 17; Cin Za Do Shoute "Damna Changa Lawmthu Sawina," *El-Bethel Magazine*, 5/43, (November, 1993): Rev. G. K. Nang, "Testimony," *El-Bethel Magazine* 5/41 (September, 1993); Tinting Vaiphei, "Testimony," *El-Bethel Magazine* 4/37, (May, 1993): 9-11.

193 Rev. Avum Haolai, "Songpijang leh Changpijang,"*El-Bethel Magazine* 7/63 (July, 1995); Ngurtinkhum Khojol, Muolhoi "Testimony," *El-Bethel Magazine* 7/63 (July, 1995); *El-Bethel Magazine* 7/62 (June 1995); Lalpiangliana Pudaite, "Bethel Report: Haflong" *El-Bethel Magazine* 7/65 (September 1995); Thankhuma Nampui, "Fiangpui El-Bethel Report," *El-Bethel Magazine* 7/67 (Nov. & Dec., 1995); H. Lalnunthara, "El-Bethel Camp Report: Harangajao Buolmoul Bagan-II N.C. Hills Assam," *El-Bethel Magazine* 7/68 (Jan., 1996): 11-13.

194 "Jalaphet-ah Kohhran adding ta," *El-Bethel Magazine* 7/61 (May, 1995); R. Biakhmingthanga, "Jalaphet- ah Inthlanna Dangdai neih ani," *El-Bethel Magazine* 6/51 (July, 1994): 15-16.

195 K. Hawla, "El-Bethel Harhna"..., 550.

196 The letter To the Team leader of El-Bethel Team from the Secretary El-Bethel Camp at Laisong (Naga village), Dated 24th February 1996, *El-Bethel Magazine* 7/70 (March, 1996): 8-9.

197 "Publication Thuhma," K. Lalhmingliana, *El-Bethel Camp Sermon* ..., v.

worshiped together and cry together to the Lord at the camp. The Chief Minister of Mizoram Mr & Mrs Lalthanhawla with six other cabinet ministers were also among the campers.[198] No special care was given to them. This shows that there was equality in the life of the people.

The El-Bethel Revival movement reformed[199] and changed the spiritual life of the families[200] as well as the social life of Mizoram; peace was restored.[201] The Bethel revival movement was directly associated to the church.[202]

During the Revival movement, Lockup was empty, and jail was nearly empty,[203] crime cases and abortion cases were tremendously reduced.[204] The life of the society was very peaceful.[205] All people were treated equally and everybody was humble and life was wonderful. So, because of this great and wonderful result in the society, D.C. of Aizawl District, L. Tochhawng, I.A.S sent letters of thanksgiving and admiration to the speaker of the El-Bethel Team on 10th June 1990.[206] Most of the El-Bethel camp was supported physically

---

198 C. L. Ruala, Liansuama, S. Hiato, Vanlalnghaka, H. Thansanga, Saikapthianga. "El-Bethel Vangin Mizoram Sorkhar Kalphung abuai," *Lentlang Weekly News* 2/4 (February 16-22, 1990): 8. It is questionable that how the Ministers can spare their valuable time for the Camp. Vanneihtluanga Interviewed on 19th May 2006 at his Lengzem Office, Chanmari.

199 Upa C. Sangzuala, "Kum 1990Mizoram," *Kristian Tlangau* LXXIX/950 (December, 1990), 29.

200 The Study Commission Report of Aizawl Theological College Faculty towards the Bethel Revival, p. 4 (Unpublished).

201 *Harhna,* Vol. XVI, Sep. 5. 1990, 2.

202 Zorinkimi Pa, "Bethel hi Engang in nge I Ngaih," *Sakeibaknei* 1/295 (April 3, 1990): 5.

203 K. Hawla Sailo, "El-Bethel Harhna"..., 557; Harhna, Vol. XVI, (Sept. 5. 1990): 2.

204 "Bethel Thunawi," *El-Bethel Magazine,* 2/14 (June, 1991), 15.

205 The Study Commission Report of Aizawl Theological College Faculty..., 4.

206 K. Hawla Sailo, "El Bethel Harhna"..., 557; L. Tochhong, IAS, D. C., Aizawl, "El-Bethel Evangelical Team Chunga Lawmthu," *El-Bethel Magazine* 1/4 (July, 1990), 13.

by the Mizoram Government.[207] Such kind of relationship[208] and involvement of the government was very rare in the past Gospel Camp history. But many government officers misused their vehicles to go to camp, which is beyond official duty.[209] There was also division in the family.[210]

6. Problems Faced by K. Hminga

6.1. Problems in Getting Acceptance in the Church: The churches in Mizoram were very careful about inviting unknown speakers in their churches. They believed the independent preachers were really hindrance to the churches.[211] There were many assumptions even upon K. Hminga.[212] On 15th May 1989, he went to Electric Veng P. C. (Aizawl) in search of a chance for his preaching ministry,[213] but his request was refused.[214] Even the church committee did not recognize their ministry to the alcoholics and drug addicts in this local church area,[215] because the church did not know his theology, his method of teachings since at that time he was new to them.

---

207 K. Hawla Sailo, "El- Bethel Harhna"..., 564.

208 Frank Kurschner Pelkmann, "Mizoram ka hmuh dan," *Kristian Tlangau* LXXIX/9969 (July, 1992), 23.

209 "Bethel leh Sorkar office te," *Sakeibaknei* 1/284 (February 20, 1990), 9.

210 "Bethel na ah an Nu lam vangin an inthen," *Forum* 1/9 (March-April 27-3, 1990), 3.

211 Many independent preachers preached different doctrines, some of the church members are attracted and later they became sectarian e.g. Tlira and his followers, emerging after the 1913 revival, Lalchhungkua (The royal household of life)(1966), Zion Church of God- Israel (1970) Lalzawna and his followers (1972), The Church of faith (1977). Rev. H. Zalawma, "The Role of Doctrinal Preaching in The Mizoram Presbyterian Church to Counter Sectarianism" (M. Th. Thesis, Senate of Serampore College, 1992).

212 Especially his method, Bethel (offering prayer in the jungle) is new, the Seeds of Faith was compared to indulgence, and the money of The Seeds of Faith was used for his family purpose. *Autobiography of Lalhmingliana...*, 46.

213 *Autobiography of Lalhmingliana...*, 34.

214 V. L. Zaikima, *Ka Tla Fai Ta...*, 74; *Autobiography of Lalhmingliana...*, 34.

215 *Autobiography of Lalhmingliana...*, 34.

In Aug.1989 after the camp at Muallungthu,[216] K. Hminga received invitation from Sialsuk for Camp;[217] K. Hminga planned to go there on 11th Sept. after camp at Maubuang.[218] By knowing their plan to go to Sialsuk by leaving the existing Camp programme in Sateek pastorate, the pastor of Sateek pastorate, Rev. Darchungnunga, wrote to him stating: *"Are you planning to leave the small villages after having Camp only in the big churches? You, the 'Eastern people'*[219] *are not trustworthy to co-operate in the ministry.*"[220] After a few days while they were in the Maubuang church, another letter from Rev. Chawnghranga[221] was received. The letter was written on 26th August 1989. It mentions that:

> ... I never heard of a minister like you, who does not respect the church and God; we expect that you are coming. But you avoid coming. If you need vehicle tell us, you are making the people of the church upset. We do not regard you as reliable to have preaching ministry in our pastorate... we will never correspond to you any more. [222]

After receiving the above letters, K. Hminga was really astonished; he wrote to his wife stating the following words:

> The one who called Abraham to offer his son in Moreh[223] was the same God who told him not to hurt the child, God was the one who rescued the Israelites from the bondage of slavery but He himself was the one who hardened the heart of Pharaoh. Jesus was the one who ordered to bring the sword for those who have; but he is the one who ordered to

216 Muallungthu is one of the churches under Sateek pastorate.

217 Sialsuk is different pastorate under Mizoram Presbyterian Church.

218 Maubuang is one of the churches under the pastorate of Sateek.

219 Eastern people can mean the people from Burma, since they are on the eastern side of Mizoram.

220 *Autobiography of Lalhmingliana...*, 40.

221 Rev. Chawnghranga was the pastor in charge of Sialsuk Pastorate.

222 *Autobiography of Lalhmingliana...*,41, V.L Zaikima, *Ka Tla Fai Ta...*, 75, 76.

223 "The land of Moriah," mentioned in Gen 22:2, where God sent Abraham to sacrifice his son, Isaac, on one of the hills in the region.

> keep the sword back. God is the one who sent me to Sialsuk, but he is the one who is obstructing my way. It is really difficult to know the rule of the Lord for the servant.[224]

The above incident happened due to love and anxiety of their respective members and ministries but they were from different perspectives and misunderstanding. But later it was settled and he was invited to preach again in the Sateek pastorate.

K. Hminga was not accepted by the churches in Aizawl city. Meanwhile one of the elders in Electric Veng P. C. invited him to preach in their church on 9th October, 1989.[225] The church was full of people eagerly waiting to hear from him. He was in the pulpit ready to preach[226] but one letter arrived from the pastor-in-charge rejecting the preaching of K. Hminga; then the Chairman announced that 'he was not allowed to preach' and he came down from the pulpit.[227]

On the next day on 10th October, 1989 (Sunday), one of the church elders of Khatla P. C. Aizawl informed him to preach at the afternoon service (1:30 PM) and evening service (6 PM) in their church.[228] When the time came for the service at 1:30 PM, the church was overflowing with people.[229] The service started; while he was approaching the pulpit for preaching, he was informed to go back and he was not allowed to preach.[230] After the service was

224 V. L. Zaikima, *Ka Tla Fai Ta…*, 79. *Autobiography of Lalhmingliana…*, 41.

225 *Autobiography of Lalhmingliana…*, 42.

226 Ibid.

227 *Autobiography of Lalhmingliana…*, 42.

228 Ibid.

229 Ibid., 43.

230 According to K. Hminga *Autobiography of K. Lalhmingliana*, p., 43, it was due to the ban of his preaching by Bungkawn Pastorate. Stating the announcement of the chairman that "Our preacher of today is banned by our Pastorate Standing Committee to preach, so he is not allowed to preach today, let the appointed person preach." But according to V. L Zaikima, V. L Zaikima, *Ka Tla Fai Ta…*, 80, the reason was that he was not accepted by one of the church elders named Upa R. Lalluna of Khatla P. C. The word of V. L. Zaikima is acceptable because Harmon PC was also under the Bungkawn Pastorate along with Khatla PC, if the Pastorate Standing Committee banned the preaching of K. Hminga, of El-Bethel team, Harmon P. C. would not allow him to preach in their Church that evening.

over the reaction of the people was very severe in the premises of the church.[231] Some were shouting, "If he is not allowed to preach in the church, let us establish a new Bethel church."[232] Later K. Hminga could control the severe feelings through humility.[233] But he preached in the Harmon P. C. in the evening worship service.[234] The pressure from the people was very great but due to the caution and experiences of the church, he was not easily engaged to preach in the church.

Aizawl city was still off bounds to their Team, but the pressure was enormous so clandestinely camp at Sateek was organised during 12th-17th Oct., 1989 by Electric Veng P. C.[235] So due to the massive pressure[236] from the members of the church it was organized without the permission of Chanmari Pastorate Standing Committee (CPSC). Many members from Chanmari pastorates attended the camp.[237] This proves that the spiritual thirst and eagerness of the members of the churches was massive and vast. While the Team were in Sateek, Rev. Darchungnunga stated that "although the door of the Aizawl city castle may be closed, but we shall shoot with cannon from Sateek Pastorate and it will collapse."[238]

The door for his preaching ministry in the Aizawl city was closed for him. For this K. Hminga blamed the Pastors and other revival speakers and stated that: "...I remember that by accumulating my various weak points I was clogged-up by the Joint sitting of the city

---

231 An interviewed with V. L. Zaikima on 27 April 2006, at Lengchhawn Press.

232 *Autobiography of Lalhmingliana...*, 44.

233 He shouted to the people accepting that it was happen under the permission of God, one day the city of Aizawl will be collapsed. *Autobiography of Lalhmingliana...*, 44.

234 Harmon Presbyterian Church was under the Bungkawn Pastorate along with Khatla Presbyterian Church.

235 *Autobiography of Lalhmingliana...*, 45. This is one of the churches under Chanmari Pastorate.

236 Upa Hmingthanga, elder of Electric Veng Presbyterian Church, interviewed on 6.5.2006 in his home.

237 Ibid.

238 K. Hawla Sailo, "El Bethel Harhna"...,557

Pastors and Revival Speakers... the churches of the city wish for the fruits but they reject the stem."[239]

Later, after having Camp at Darlung village on 30th Oct.-4th Nov. 1989 his team was invited to the thanksgiving service at Harmon Church, Aizawl, and they arrived on 8th Nov., 1989.[240] But the order came to the church committee that having Thanksgiving Service with K. Hminga was restricted by the Bungkawn Pastorate Standing Committee.[241] K. Hminga met the pastor in-charge of that area, Rev. Z. T. Sangkhuma, and requested him to organise open discussion on misunderstandings between the El-Bethel Team, speaker and the churches. Then Rev Z. T. Sangkhuma called the meeting; four pastors[242] and many church leaders[243] came together on 10th Nov., 1989 in the residence of M. C. Lalfala.[244] Rev. Lalchama chaired the meeting. The attitude was diverse before the conclusion was made. Rev. Z. T. Sangkhuma departed from the meeting,[245] but the meeting kept going on. Rev. Laltanliana states, "There was a time that God used evangelists; I would like to use them in my pastorate before they lose their saltiness."[246] And he also stated that, "I will blow the ram horn in my pastorate, and the wall of Jericho will collapse."[247] Then K. Hminga was engaged in the Luangmual Pastorate at Chawlhhmun

---

239 *Autobiography of Lalhmingliana...*, 45.

240 Ibid., 47.

241 Ibid.

242 The four pastors are Rev. Z. T. Sangkhuma, C. Laltanliana, Lalchama and Thangpuiliana. V. L. Zaikima, *Ka Tla Fai Ta...*, 81.

243 Elders from Bungkawn Pastorate. V. L. Zaikima, *Ka Tla Fai Ta...*, 81.

244 V.L Zaikima, *Ka Tla Fai Ta...*, 81.

245 *Autobiography of Lalhmingliana...*, 48.

246 K. Hawla Sailo, " El Bethel Harhna ... ,545; V. L. Zaikima, *Ka Tla Fai Ta ...*, 82; *In the Autobiography of Lalhmingliana..*. , 48; the statement of Laltanliana was little bit different "There was a time that God uses evangelists; because I would like to used El-Bethel Team first in my pastorate before they loose their saltiness."

247 V. L. Zaikima, *Ka Tla Fai Ta ...*, 82; Rev. Laltanliana interviewed on 29.4.2006 at Chanmari.

during 17th-27th Nov., 1989.[248] This was the beginning of the city ministry. Still there was confusion among the churches.

But after preaching in the Mission Veng church[249] during 26th and 27th Dec., 1989[250] the suspicion was reduced and many churches in the Aizawl city were eager to utilize him.[251]

From the above point it is seen that he was really facing problems of criticism, suspicion, and rejection; at the same time people favoured him and his preaching was really attractive to them. Because of this while he was having Gospel Camp outside Aizawl city; people pursued him entering his camp even from various churches of Aizawl city.

6.2. Failure in Mentoring the Team Members: Whenever they went to have El-Bethel Camp, the newly converted like, alcoholics, drug addicts, and commercial sex workers, and many other types of volunteers, male and female, accompany the team to share their testimonies,[252] and to sing songs.[253] But their misconduct anguished the administration and often faced complaints from some people. The answers of the respondent in the interviews and questionnaires were same to this regard that the administration was not strict at all. There was always quarreling among them. Even after eight years of experiences, problems still existed. While K. Hminga was at Chhiahtlang along with his team, in K. Hminga's letter on 18.6.1995 to K. Hawla, K. Hminga mentioned that "the members of the team could not still avoid quarreling and condemning one another."[254] This highlighted that the interpersonal relationship of the team members was poor, and they always created trouble. The

248 V. L Zaikima, *Ka Tla Fai Ta…,* 82.

249 This is highly regarded and influential, since this church is the head quarter church from the time of Western Missionaries.

250 K. Hawla Sailo, "El-Bethel Harhna"…, 545.

251 C. Vanlallawma, *Bethel Revival …,* 6.

252 Lalhriatpuii, *Ka Damna Isua …,* 69, 81, 84.

253 Ibid., 71, 83.

254 The letter of K. Lalhmingliana, from Chhiahtlang on 18.6.1995 to K. Hawla (unpublished).

word, "Your co-workers in the midst of disparaging and praise" was always the concluding sentence in K. Hminga's letters.[255]

II. El-Bethel Team In Chanmari and Dawrpui Vengthar Pastorates

1. Background

After separation from the team of C. Lalchungnunga, K. Hminga with his team moved to preach to N. Khawbung village and the neighbouring villages.[256] It was successful and truly revived the people. This was the first preaching tour with his new team.

1.1. Preaching Ministry to the Rural Area: As William Steward stated, "a minister of the gospel has received not only an inner call but also an outward commission in the Church to preach the Word of God,"[257] K. Hminga had his preaching ministry at Bawngkawn[258] P. C. Meanwhile, he was invited by four churches.[259] He went to Vaphai Church and stayed for 1988 Christmas where enormous revival took place. Revival on such large scale had never happened before in this church.[260] El-Bethel camp was organized at Farkawn and here putting stick[261] was started. After this they had camp in the E. Lungdar village during 8th-24th February 1989. There were 1275 campers, a great revival took place and the movement was very

255 The letter of K. Lalhmingliana, from Chhiahtlang on 18.6.1995 to K. Hawla (unpublished); the letter of K. Lalhmingliana, from Champhai on 11.5.1995 to K. Hawla (unpublished).

256 The villages are Sesih, Leisenzo, Bulfek, Salvation Army of Kahrawt Veng, Champhai Zotlang, Kelkang, Buang, Bungzung, S. Khawbung, Zawlsei, Khuangthing, and Samthang. V. L. Zaikima, *Ka Tla Fai Ta…*, 72- 73.

257 William Steward, *The Nature and Calling of the Church* (Madras: CLS, 1958), 161.

258 Bawngkawn is one of the Presbyterian Churches in Aizawl City.

259 Sairang, Sateek, E. Lungdar, Vaphai churches, V. L. Zaikima, *Ka Tla Fai Ta…*, 73.

260 V. L. Zaikima, *Ka Tla Fai Ta…*, 73.

261 To count /know the exact numbers of the person who are in Bethel prayer from the RV.

broad and influential. A memorial stone of Bethel was erected by the church, and inscribed:[262]

BETHEL

"*This is the place that the Lord answers the prayers of the sinners, Let it remain Bethel. Amen.*" E. Lungdar Presbyterian Church.

10.6. 1989.

On receiving invitation, they moved to Mualcheng PC. And as usual practice, Ministers Camp, General Camp, *Lang* camp (meaning: Day camp/attending in the camp without staying the night in the camp) were organised. After Mualcheng they conducted camp in Leng, Chalrang churches in April 1989 and in Tachhip Church on 20th May 1989.[263] Camp in the Aibawk and Phulpui of Sateek pastorate followed. Then they had camp in Muallungthu. Many people came for camp from Aizawl, but they were refused by the organiser.[264] This showed the power of his revival preaching. Afterward another camp was organized at Maubuang 26th August 1989, campers 700; 400 of them are from Aizawl city. At Thiak camp was organized there are, 500 campers; out of 500 campers, 300 are from Aizawl city. Camp was organised at Hmuifang, then camp at Sateek followed during 17th-21st October 1989, campers 300 and Rs. 5,468.00 was received as Seeds of Faith.[265] Another camp at Darlung village followed during 30th October - 4th November 1989 there are 704 campers.[266] V. L. Zaikima says, "Even before the entry into Aizawl city, revival movement really shuddered and influenced the entire atmosphere of Mizoram." [267]

1.2. Entry in to Aizawl City: The first Major El-Bethel camp in the city of Aizawl was organised by Luangmual Pastorate. The 40th sitting of The Luangmual Pastorate Standing Committee on

262 V. L. Zaikima, *Ka Tla Fai Ta…*, 74.

263 Ibid., 75.

264 Ibid.

265 V. L. Zaikima, *Ka Tla Fai Ta…*, 80.

266 Ibid., 82.

267 C. Vanlallawma, *Bethel Revival …*, 4.

29th November 1989 resolved to organize El-Bethel Camp[268] and it was implemented at Luangmual Chawlhhmun during 17th-27th November 1989.[269] Campers were 365; donation for the Seeds of Faith was Rs. 21,641. 00. At Aibawk during 28th November-2nd December 1989, campers were 1800.[270] At Tanhril during 12th December 1989-1st January 1990, campers were 4922, donation for Seeds of Faith 2, 80, 700.00. At Chite Lui Arm Veng church organized camp during 4th-13th January 1990 Campers were 6600, for the Seeds of Faith Rs. 2,70,233.00 was received.[271] After this the camp was organised by Arm Veng church; Chanmari and Dawrpui Vengthar Pastorates organized a joint Camp.

2. The Committee of Chanmari and Dawrpui Vengthar Pastorates for the Organization of El-Bethel Camp

2.1. The Beginning: In the sitting of the 8th Dawrpui Vengthar Pastorate Standing Committee (DVPSC) on 27th December 1989 10A.M. at Pastor Quarters. Four churches[272] proposed to organize El- Bethel camp in the pastorate level, and it was resolved that due to the uncertainty of time it was not possible at a pastorate level but churches were allowed to organise.[273]

In the meantime the 127th CPSC sitting on 30th December 1989; agenda No. 2 resolved to organize El-Bethel camp and the secretary was entrusted to proceed the resolution to be able to produce a concrete proposal in their next sitting at 2 P.M. of the same day.[274] In the 2 PM sitting, the secretary reported that DVPSC reserved

268 The minute of The 40th sitting of The Luangmual Pastorate Standing Committee on 29th .11.1989. (Unpublished).

269 V. L. Zaikima, *Ka Tla Fai Ta…*, 82.

270 Ibid.

271 Ibid., 84.

272 Dawrpui Vengthar, Vaivakawn, Chawnpui and Kanan churches

273 The 8th Dawrpui Vengthar Pastorate Standing Committee Minute book of 1989, Mizoram Presbyterian Church.

274 The 127th Chanmari Pastorate Standing Committee Minute, book 1989, Mizoram Presbyterian Church.

the El-Bethel Team for the next Camp;[275] so the committee resolved to contact the DVPSC.[276] Accordingly they were contacted by the secretary. At the sitting of the 128th CPSC on 3rd January 1990 at 7 AM,[277] Upa Lalhluna representative of DVPSC gave reports of their actions and the date of the camp was fixed on 15th January 1990. So, this Committee resolved to set up 'Organizing Committee' and the Committee proposed six[278] names to represent Chanmari Pastorate in the organizing committee:

This committee assigned the Office Bearers for the Organizing Committee:

1. Chairman	:	Upa K. Chaldailova
2. Vice Chairman	:	Upa Hmingthanga
3. Secretary	:	Upa Lalhluna
4. Assistant Secretary	:	Upa F. Lallura
5. Treasurer	:	Upa Chhunkhuma
		Pu. P. B. Rosanga

In the sitting of the 9th DVPSC on 6th January, 1990 at 1 PM the committee resolved to accept the proposals from Chanmari Pastorate, and proposed nine (9) names for joint committee members.[279] After this, there was mutual understanding and the responsible secretaries took initiatives for the smooth running of the Organizing Committee.

275 The Luangmual Pastorate organized El-Bethel Camp on those days from 12.12.1989-1.1.1990.

276 The 127th Chanmari Pastorate Standing Committee Minute book 1989, Mizoram Presbyterian Church.

277 The 128th Chanmari Pastorate Standing Committee Minute book, 1989, Mizoram Presbyterian Church.

278 Upa Lalhrangluaia of Chanmari, Upa Hmingthanga of Electric Veng, Upa R. Rozinga of Ramthar Veng, Upa F. Lallura of Electric Veng, Upa Chhunkhuma of Ramthar Veng, Upa L. Rozika of Electric Veng, The 128th Chanmari Pastorate Standing Committee Minute book. Mizoram Presbyterian Church.

279 Upa Lalhluna Vaivakawn, Upa. Kapthuama Kanan, Upa. R. Dawngliana Chawnpui, Pu. P. B. Rosanga, Churches representatives are: Upa. Lalawia of Hmunthar Church, Upa. C. Rozama of Tuikual Church, Upa. R. Lalliana of Dinthar Church, Upa. P. Lalzuala of Dawrpui Vengthar and Upa C. Makliana of Zotlang. The 9th Dawrpui Vengthar Pastorate Standing Committee Minute book of 1990, Mizoram Presbyterian Church.

2.2. The Organizing Committee with El-Bethel Evangelical Team: As the Organizing Committee were created by the two Pastorates. All the actions were in their hand. If they needed support, the Standing Committees were ready to help them any time. The Organizing Committee members were:[280]

1. Upa Lalhrangluaia of Chanmari
2. Upa Hmingthanga of Electric Veng
3 Upa R. Rozinga of Ramthar Veng
4. Upa F. Lallura of Electric Veng
5. Upa Chhunkhuma of Ramthar Veng
6. Upa L. Rozika of Electric Veng
7. Upa Lalkunga of Chanmari West[281]
8. Upa. Lalawia of Hmunthar Church
9. Upa. C. Rozama of Tuikual Church
10. Upa. R. Lalliana of Dinthar Church
11. Upa P. Lalzuala of Dawrpui Vengthar
12. Upa C. Makliana of Zotlang

The Organizing Committee and some of the El-Bethel Team members met together regarding their future ministry. The committee appointed representatives for the members of Security, Food, Transportation, Lodging, Sanitation, Water, Electricity and Medical Department in this sitting.

3. The Camp

The name of the place is called Tanhril. The place of camp was around four to five kilometres away from the area of the organizers. Camp was organized in the Government Sporting complex, and a big worship hall called 'Pandal,' was used by the previous Camp Organizers.[282]

280 Dawrpui Vengthar Pastorate Standing Committee Minute book of 1990, Mizoram Presbyterian Church. Chanmari Pastorate Standing Committee Minute book of 1990.

281 The name Upa Lalkunga was not in the minute book of The 128th Chanmari Pastorate Standing Committee Minute, but his name was added later, and he was an active participant in the committee. An interview with Upa Lalkunga on 6.5.2006 at his house.

282 Luangmual Pastorate organized El-Bethel camp on 12.12.1989-1.1.1990, just before this camp was started. And all the building and materials were spare for

But due to increase of campers the organising committee borrowed tarpaulins from Mizoram Transport Department and the area was extended to occupy more than 3000 campers. Camp was organized two times, for two types of groups.

3.1. Ministers Camp (Rawngbawltu Camp): This first camp was for the ministers, during 15th-18th January 1990. Here 'ministers' does not mean only ordained persons but even those who have responsibilities and particular appointment in various church activities.[283] There were 2483 campers and Rs. 1,72,939 in the Seeds of Faith in this Camp.[284]

3.2. General Camp: General Camp was held during 22nd -26th January 1990. This camp was for all types of people**.** It was for the members of the organizing churches, members of other denominations, Christians and non-Christians. But since it was organized by the two pastorates, special preference was given to the church members of the two pastorates due to the limitation of seats and accommodation. But some entered without tickets. 3000 tickets were distributed equally to the two pastorates but there were much more than 3000 campers. The exact number of campers is not known.[285]

4. Result of the El-Bethel Camp at Tanhril

After the camp was over a great revival was taking place in all the churches of the two pastorates. But due to limitation of seats in the camp many members could not get chance for camp. Fortunately Khatla P. C. gave them 500 seats[286] for the two pastorates. The 130th sitting of CPSC on 29th January, '90, Agenda No. 1 resolved to apply

---

this camp and most of them are reused.

283 This included pastors, elders, Sunday school teachers, preachers, Wednesday night topic openers, worship opener (doing Bible reading and prayers), song leaders, offering collectors, different Committee Members, women committee member, and youth committee members.

284 V. L. Zaikima, *Ka Tla Fai Ta…*, 79; *Autobiography of Lalhmingliana…*, 85.

285 Upa. Lalhluna, Secretary of the Organizing Committee report to the writer of this thesis on 21st May 2006.in black and white, unpublished.

286 Just after the El-Bethel camp was organized by Chanmari and Dawrpui Vengthar pastorates, Khatla church took over the El-Bethel Team to organize the El-Bethel camp.

for another 1000 seats for the two pastorates.[287] Churches began to organize early Morning Prayer service after this camp.[288] The 131st sitting of CPSC on 3rd Feb. 1990, Agenda no. 2 reviewed the past camp and stated:

> It revived the life of the people, it drew many backsliders to the church, and many *pawlchhuak* (abandoner of the churches and some people who joined some sectarian groups) are revived and returned to the church, this is really beneficial for the church. At the same time there are some point's needs to be careful and have lots of responsibility to look after the new converts and to encourage each church to work for it.[289]

The statement shows that they were really positive. Forgiveness to one another was taking place to the debtors, between spouses, fathers and children. Many members were drawn to the churches, all the churches were full. Relationships were restored, and there was no discrimination between the rich and the poor; mothers, fathers, boys and girls, young and old, male and female gathered and the message of love and concerns of sinners prevailed, compassion for the poor and humility was achieved. No discriminations in church denominations.[290] Singing and dancing in the worship service became the habit of the people. Some church[291] buildings were extended due to the increase of Church goers.[292] This reminds us the words of Charles Finney, "There was a great movement and many lives changed."[293]

---

287 The minute of the 130th sitting of Chanmari Pastorate Standing Committee on 29th Jan. '90.

288 "Lawrkhawm," *Darthlalang*, Silver jubilee Special Issue, (Aizawl: An organ of Tuikual Branch KTP 2005), 32.

289 The Minute of The 131st sitting of Chanmari Pastorate Standing Committee on 3rd February 1990, Agenda no. 2. (Unpublished).

290 C. Vanlallawma, *Bethel Revival* ..., 6.

291 Like Chanmari West, Electric Veng, Ramthar Veng churches.

292 Upa. Lalkunga interviewed on 6.5.2006 at his residence Chanmari West.

293 Brian H. Edwards, *Revival! A people Saturated with God* (Darlington: Evangelical Press, 1990), 31.

Didakhe states that, "A great revival was taking place since the last part of last year. Many people were revived and received personal knowledge of salvation, spiritual growth in Christian life ... the inner fellowship of the Holy Spirit, humility was articulated, and the enormous ecstatic experience was seen."[294] *Kristian Tlangau*[295] Editorial also highlights the results of El-Bethel camp under the heading of 'The Storm of El- Bethel' and states that:

> From the month of December (1989) onwards there is a storm of El-Bethel around Aizawl city, thousands of thousands people attended the camp at Tanhril and Chite. They return with full of joy receiving the new inspiration of the Holy Spirit, the attendance in the church services has enormously increased. Fighting in the streets, vehicle accidents are very rare during Christmas and New Year; it is an acceptable fact that the storm of El-Bethel blew them away.[296]

In these two Camps[297] the surplus money of the Seeds of Faith after recovering all the expenditures in the camp was around Rs. 2,00,000.00. From this Rs. 1,00,000.00 was donated to Aizawl Theological College. Rs. 50,000. 00 was donated to the Bible Society, Aizawl Auxiliary. And 25 tarpaulins were purchased to replace the old, which were borrowed from the Government and used in the Camp.[298] Some portion was also donated to support the El-Bethel Team.[299]

---

294 "Harhna Aizawl Khawpui leh Mizoram ah," *Didakhe,* 19/1 (January-February, 1990): 25.

295 Since 1911. This journal is the Official organ of the Mizoram Presbyterian Church (Monthly Journal).

296 C. Sangzuala, "El-Bethel Thli," *Kristian Tlangau* LXXVIII/39 (February, 1990): 6.

297 Ministers camp and General camp.

298 Upa Lalhluna, Secretary of the Organizing Committee reports to the author, 21st May 2006.

299 K. Hawla Sailo, "El- Bethel Harhna"..., 548.

5. Problems in the Tanhril El-Bethel Camp

Ticket system was introduced for better administration but many people entered in the camp without having tickets. This disturbed the administration in the camp. Many people were sent back due to limitation of seats, and getting tickets was difficult. This caused the suicide of Mr. Lungmuana H/o Thanchhingi of Chanmari West Presbyterian Church. The suicide note found in his pocket mentioned that he did it because he could not get the ticket for Camp.[300] Since he was from the organizing area his death affected the atmosphere of the particular church. Upa Lalkunga of Chanmari West Presbyterian Church says, "Mostly people think that getting a ticket was like having the ticket to heaven."[301]

Inside the Camp one alcoholic from Bawngkawn locality[302] died due to withdrawal symptoms[303] According to Upa Lalhluna, the secretary of the Organizing committee, 'his death did not much disturb the camp programme, but being organizers we did what we must do.'[304]

After this camp, ban of using Government tarpaulin was submitted to the Government authority.[305] This shows that the Government was not happy about using its properties.

III. The Role of the Revival Committee of Mizoram Presbyterian Church

1. Origin

Revivals often took place in Mizoram churches from 1903.[306] It affected the life of the church in positive and negative ways. Because

300 Upa. Lalhluna, Secretary of the Organizing Committee…, 3. (Unpublished) Upa. Lalkunga of Chanmari West on 6th May 2006.

301 Upa Lalkunga interviewed on 6th-5th 2006 in his residence.

302 "Bethel Camp ah Drugs man ani,"*Lentlang* 11/11 (March, 1990): 4.

303 Upa Lalhluna, Secretary of the Organizing Committee…, 2.

304 Ibid.

305 Ibid., 3.

306 The revival in 1906, 1913, 1916, 1919, 1926, 1936, 1937 Vanlalchhuanawma, *Christianity and Subaltern Culture: Revival Movement as a Cultural Response to Westernization in Mizoram* (Madras: ISPCK, 2006), 164, 196, 231, 237, 320,

of this, in 1949, North Lushai Assembly Standing Committee published "Revival Guide/ Manual of-1949"[307] called "Harhna Hruaina-1949."[308] In 1976 Synod Meeting, it was resolved to establish "Committee of Evangelism,"[309] but after studying the concern and related ministries, the Synod Executive Committee (SEC) proposed the name "Synod Revival Committee" in 1977 Synod Meeting and it was accepted by the floor. In this proposal, numbers of Committee Members, term and conditions, power, duties and functions were included. The first committee was on 26 November, 1978 under the chairmanship of Rev. Zairema.[310] According to the 1978 Synod it was under the chairmanship of the Moderator of the Presbyterian Church Synod. [311]

2. Development

The first Synod Revival Programme was organised during 27th-29th January, 1979 at Hualngohmun. During this time independent preachers were already there but a revival speaker were not yet appointed. Many independent preachers were travelling in and outside Mizoram; so Synod Revival Committee (SRC) called them and organized seminar for these preachers. Full time workers were also appointed by the Synod; Rev. L. Z. Zolawma (1980-1985) was the first time full time as Revival Worker in this department.[312] In

369, 384; Rev. Lalsawma, *Kristian Thurin Zirna Bu* (Aizawl: Synod Literature and Publication Board, 1998), 101, 105, 110, 112, 119, 113, 114, 116, 119.

307 Vanlalchhuanawma translated *Harhna Hruaina-1949* as *Revival Guide/ Manual of-1949*; Vanlalchhuanawma, *Christianity and Subaltern Culture...*, 449.

308 "Harhna Hruaina," Upa Dr. R. L. Thanmawia (Ed) *Harhna Mizoram Revival Centenary Souvenir (1906-2006)* (Aizawl: Synod Revival Committee, 2006), 693-702.

309 1976 Synod, Agenda, General No. 35 proposed from the Chhimphei Presbytery Meeting of 1976 cited by Rev. F. Lalrinnunga, "Synod Revival Committee Report," *Harhna Mizoram Revival Centenary Souvenir (1906-2006)* (Aizawl: Synod Revival Committee, 2006), 703.

310 *Mizoram Presbyterian Kohhran Department Chanchin* (Aizawl: Synod Publication Board, 1987), 177.

311 1978 Synod, Gen 12 (2).

312 *Mizoram Presbyterian Kohhran Department Chanchin ...*, 178.

1995-1997 the department was upgraded; the worker was called Synod Revival Co-ordinator. From 1998 till today the name of the post is called Synod Revival Director.[313] He was assisted by other staff in his office. The sitting of the 180th SEC, Gen.60 of 7th-9th February 2001 revised the guidelines of Revival Department and resolved that the teams were not allowed to stay more than 12 days in a particular church,[314] and were not allowed to prepare separate songbooks; and the appointment of Revival speaker was temporary and should be appointed yearly by the office.

3. Contribution to the Churches

The SRC appointed speakers from various independent preachers in the earlier days, but now mostly appoints through local churches. They were helpful to the churches to revive the spiritual life of the congregation. These preachers mainly formed a Team or a Group; the sizes are different from one to another. All the Revival Teams were enrolled in the office of Synod Revival office. Whenever the churches request to the Revival Department for Revival Crusade, Camp, or Campaign,[315] Director appoints suitable speakers from the list of the speakers in consultation with them. Then after the church resolved and set the date and time, the speakers and his team were sent to the respective church and fulfilled their purposes. The Revival office also bears the travelling allowances and daily allowances for six members[316] for five days while they were engaged in the revival programme.[317] Rev. F. Lalrinnunga stated that:

> The ministry of Synod Revival department bears lovely fruits. Wherever the ministry was organized, the offering in the church was increased; many people are drawing to the

---

313 Rev. F. Lalrinnunga, "Synod Revival" ..., 707.

314 The fifth Book of Synod Revival, Major Guidelines of Camp and Campaign, Mizoram Presbyterian Church (Aizawl: Synod Revival Committee, 1982, 2002), 8-9.

315 *Mizoram Presbyterian Kohhran Department Chanchin...*, 179-180.

316 Rev, Dr. R. Lalbiakmawia, ed., *Synod Department –te Inkahhruaina*, (Aizawl: Synod Multipurpose Training Centre, 2005), 82-83.

317 Rev. F. Lalrinnunga, "Synod Revival" ..., 708.

church, although it is not perfect but till today God uses this ministry to revive the weak in the church.[318]

4. Revival Department of Mizoram Presbyterian Church and El-Bethel Team

There were many good results of the campaign and camp in the church history; at the same time there were false preachers that created problems in the churches.[319] From the past experiences the Mizoram Presbyterian Church, Synod was very much careful and strict in the recognition of independent preachers in Mizoram. Many independent preachers disturbed the churches, and formed some sectarian groups from the members of the church.[320] Because of this some steps were taken by the Synod. The Synod Department Study Commission's instruction, (1997 Synod, Minute, p. 94, ATC No. 8)[321] Aizawl Theological College (ATC) staff studied the preaching ministry of K. Hminga, Speaker of El-Bethel Team from December 1989-April 1990. Some of his methods and teachings were new to the church, and the revival movement was very persuasive, powerful, and covered the entire state of Mizoram and the neighbouring states.

While the El-Bethel team was studied by the faculty of ATC, the speaker K. Hminga was not yet included in the list of the Revival Speakers under Synod Revival Department. The conventional practice was that only Synod Revival Speakers (SRS) were allowed to preach in the PCs in Mizoram. But K. Hminga was much favoured by the people and he was invited by the churches and pastorates,

---

318 Ibid.

319 *Mizoram Presbyterian Kohhran Department Chanchin…*, 179.

320 Rev. H. Zalawma, "The Role of Doctrinal Preaching in the Mizoram Presbyterian Church to Counter Sectarianism," (M.Th. Thesis, Submitted to the Senate of Serampore College 1992): 101.

321 The Study Commission report of 1987 proposed and entrusted the staff of Aizawl Theological College to study, the big Revival movement and their teaching and method in Mizoram which can disturb the church in Mizoram. They should submit their findings to the Pastoral Committee through Revival Committee. Synod Pastoral Committee Minute of 27.10.1990 agenda No. 21, Aizawl, Mizoram (Unpublished).

disobeying the existing principles. This created problems in the church. So, in the 68th sitting of SRC on 17th January 1990, at 2 PM, discussed the Preaching ministry of El-Bethel team speaker K. Hminga at Agenda No.5,[322] regarding his style, method, Bethel Prayer and the Seeds of Faith. But the committee did not give any comment, positive or negative.

In the sitting of Synod Pastoral Committee on 27th October 1990 (10 AM, Agenda No. 21) the study group from ATC submitted their study report of five pages (according to 1997 Synod, Minute, p. 94, ATC No. 8), and it was read out. The committee resolved to distribute the report sheets to all the pastors and all the churches. Appreciation was given to the study group. In this report, it was noted that only up to April 1990, there were already 1,00,288 campers participated in the Bethel Camp.[323] The report was positive and concluded that this was the biggest ever Revival movement in Mizoram. The nature of this Revival movement was same like the other revivals; it was not very disturbing, but rather beneficial to the people and the church.

The 80th sitting of SRC on 14th June, 1991 Agenda No. 3 resolved to organize a special meeting with the S.R.S and ministers in the Aizawl city, and the date was fixed on 25th July 1990. This committee resolved to invite S.R.S. and 10 independent speakers;[324] among the invitees K. Hminga's name was on serial number one. This shows that he was still not yet registered among the S.R.S. Agenda No. 4 of the same committee mentioned that they received the study reports

322 Minute of the 68th Synod Revival Committee on 17.1.1990 (2:00 PM) Agenda No. 5, at Synod Committee Room, Aizawl, Mizoram.

323 The report of the study Team of Aizawl Theological College Faculty on Bethel Revival Movement, 1990: I (Unpublished).

324 1. K. Lalhmingliana, 2. Lalramliana. 3. C. Lalchungnunga of Ramhlun Venglai, 4. Speaker of Servant of God, 5. Speaker of Gospel Reapers Team, 6. Tv. Lianhmingthanga, 7. Lalzawmliani, 8. Vanlalnghaki, 9. Nithanga, 10. Tv. Zonunsanga. The minute of the 80th sitting of Synod Revival Committee on 14th June 1991 agenda No. 3, Aizawl, Mizoram.

of ATC Faculty in relation to the El-Bethel Revival movement, and resolved not to take action since it was belatedly.[325]

The date and time of inclusion of K. Hminga among the members of S.R.S is not known. In the minutes of the 117th Sitting of the SRC on 26th November 1997, the list of 48 ever ready S.R.S., includes the name of K. Hminga on Sl. No. 33.[326] And there were 22 other reserved speakers.

He was re-appointed in the next year, 1998. There were 45 speakers on the list, and K. Hminga is in Sl. No. 24.[327] He remains the S.R.S in 2001. There were 38 Speakers; his name was in Sl. No. 21, [328] and new six speakers were appointed.

In the year 2002, K. Hminga received a letter[329] from Rev. Vanlalfaka, Sr. Executive Secretary i/c Revival, Synod Office, and the letter contained the termination of his appointment as S.R.S. He was informed that the resolution was based on personal condition of health, old age and others. During this time his health was not good and he could not preach for some time.

While he was a S.R.S. he was following the rules and regulations, but due to the enormous demand of the churches, some procedures were difficult to fulfil for him. Even though many other speakers were there, he was always, requested, and even compelled by the churches to come to their church. Under such pressure, to follow the rules and procedures was a burden for him. Rev. C. Vanlalhruaia stated that, "Some complain was also upon him that he was violating the procedure, sometimes churches were annoyed with him because

325 The minute of the 80th sitting of SRC on 14th June 1991 Agenda No. 4, Aizawl, Mizoram.

326 The minute of the 117th sitting of the SRC on 26th Nov. 1997, Aizawl, Mizoram.

327 The minute of the 121st Sitting of the SRC on 28th October 1998, Aizawl, Mizoram.

328 The minute of the 133rd Sitting of the SRC on 6th February 2001, Aizawl, Mizoram.

329 The letter from Rev. Vanlalfaka S. E. S. i/c Revival, Synod Office dated 5th Feb. 2002; this letter proceeded according to the resolution of the sitting of the Revival Committee on 29th Jan. 2002.

they could not get him in their appointed time to organize El-Bethel revival camp. But as far as possible, he was following the norms and submitted the reports of his preaching ministry to the authority."[330]

IV. Summary

K. Lalhmingliana born in Mizoram migrated to Burma and again to India and lived in Champhai, Mizoram. He was an influential and famous revival preacher; because of his preaching ministry a great revival took place in all the churches of Mizoram and outside Mizoram. Before he was well known to the churches in Mizoram, he was not welcomed to the churches for some time. But, later he was renowned to the churches and most of his ministry was recognised and continuously invited by the churches. He became the most powerful instrument for the coming of revival to the churches in Mizoram. He established El-Bethel Evangelical Team, and he newly introduced Bethel Camp, Bethel Prayer, Seeds of Faith, and Ticket System in the camp. His main preaching ministry was directly related to camp method; wherever they went El-Bethel camp was organized by the churches. His ministry reached vast range of people- from commercial sex workers to pastors and church leaders; it was for all and to all churches and all denominations. A great El-Bethel Camp was organized by the joint Committee of Chanmari and Dawrpui Vengthar pastorates; through this camp a great revival took place in the two pastorates, and it really benefited the members of the churches. He was recognized by the Synod Revival Committee and he was appointed as revival speaker for about 12 years.

Through his preaching ministry many people were revived by the Holy Spirit. And his preaching was regarded as revival preaching since his preaching was the instrument of the Holy Spirit to revive the people and draw them back to the church. This shows that he was serving the Lord by doing preaching ministry as long as possible in his life time; he spent all his might, time, strength and talent to bring back the backsliders as well as preaching the gospel to the unbelievers and bring them to the Lord.

330 Rev. C. Vanlalhruaia, Ex-Moderator of the Mizoram Presbyterian Church, Synod; interviewed on 13th May 2006 in his residence.

Chapter 3

K. Lalhmingliana
His Evangelical Sermons and Their Analysis

I. Introduction

Having considered K. Lalhmingliana's preaching as evangelical preaching, the study proceeds to make an analysis of his sermons in this Chapter 3. This chapter takes up the history of the collection of the themes of sermons along with the Biblical texts and their classifications. Sermons for analysis are taken from the preaching at Tanhril Camp, organized by Chanmari and Dawrpui Vengthar Pastorates.

1. Themes and Biblical Texts of the Sermons

1.1. History of Collection

Though K. Lalhmingliana began his preaching ministry while he was in Burma, most of the sermons in Burma are not available. His preaching ministry was not regular at that time because he was in-charge of Bethel Prayer, in the team of Lalchungnunga.[331] His sermons were collected through Journal of *El-Bethel Magazine*, Vol. I, No. I, April 1990 - Issue, No. 71, April 1996, books like *El-Bethel*

331 Agape Gospel Herald Team under the leadership of C. Lalchungnunga.

Camp Sermons Vol. I., Audio Sermon Cassettes of K. Lalhmingliana, and from video cassettes and CD recordings. All the sermons were preached in Mizo dialect; English translation is not available but it is heard that the English translation is going on in America under the guidance of Mr. Rochunga Pudaite, the President of Bible for The World.[332] Some of the sermons are collected from the book which is to be published and named *'Zoram Harhna Ropui - El-Bethel Volume II' (The Great Revival in Mizoram- El-Bethel Vol. II).* All the collected sermons are in print, audio, video, and they are in Mizo dialect.

1.2. Biblical Texts and Themes

Most of the sermons were preached in the Camp. As Karl Barth says, "The only task of the preacher was to repeat what he had heard in the text of the scripture."[333] Like wise, they are repeated regularly since the Gospel Camp was organized in various places to diverse people in the North Eastern States like Mizoram, Manipur, Assam,[334] Meghalaya,[335] Tripura and Nagaland.[336] Originally sermons were preached in Mizo dialect. 70 sermons are collected in full text along with Biblical references except serial numbers 58 and 70; the sermons of K. Lalhmingliana, themes and biblical references are the following.

1. Humility-The Gospel that Reaches Sinners *(Tlawmna nun-Misualte hnen thlengphak Chanchin Tha).* Luke 5:29-32, 10:30-35, 19: 5-7.[337]

---

332 Mr. Thanchhunga interviewed on 24.4.2006 at his residence, Tuikual, Aizawl.

333 Klaas Runia "Preaching and the Work of the Holy Spirit" part 2 *The Reformed Theological Review* 60/1 (April, 2001), 30.

334 Rev. Avum Haolai, "Songpijang leh Changpijang," *El-Bethel Magazine* 7/.63 (July, 1995); Lalpiangliana Pudaite, "Bethel Report: Haflong" *El-Bethel Magazine* 7/65 (September, 1995); H. Lalnunthara, "El-Bethel Camp Report: Harangajao Buolmoul Bagan-II, N. C. Hills Assam," *El-Bethel Magazine* 7/68 (January, 1996), 11-13.

335 R. Biakhmingthanga, "Jalaphet-ah Inthlanna Dangdai neih ani (Peculiar election held in Jalaphet)," *El-Bethel Magazine* 6/51 (July, 1994), 15-16.

336 K. Hawla, "El-Bethel Harhna"..., 550.

337 K. Lalhmingliana, "Tlawmna nun- Misualte hnen thlengphak Chanchin Tha," *El-Bethel Magazine*, No. I, (April 1990): 9-12, K. Lalhmingliana, *El-Bethel*

2. The Window to the World (*Khawvel Tukverh*). II Samuel 11:1-13.[338]
3. Without the Lad *(Taitea tel lovin).* Genesis 44:30-34, Proverb 22:6, 24:11.[339]
4. The Life of a never ending Fountain. *(Tuihna Kang Ngailo Nun)* Isaiah 58:6-12.[340]
5. The Life that Negates Comforts. (*Thlamuanna duh lo nun*). Psalm 77:1-4, Matthew 7:42[341]
6. Enemy of the Cross (*Kros Hmelma*). Philippians 3:17-20.[342]
7. Extending the Tent *(Puan In zauh).* Isaiah 54:1-3.[343]
8. Prince of Peace *(Remna Lal).* Isaiah 9:6-7.[344]
9. The Life Read by All *(Mitinin an Chhiara chu).*II Corinthians3:2-6, Habakkuk 2: 2.[345]
10. The Path of the Children of the Cross *(Kraws Fate Kalkawng).* Psalm 84:1-7.[346]

Camp Sermon 1/ I (Aizawl: El-Publication Board, 1993), 1-7.

338 K. Lalhmingliana, " Khawvel Tukverh," *El-Bethel Magazine*, 1/2 (May 1990): 3-7; K. Lalhmingliana, *El- Bethel Camp Sermon* ..., 101-110.

339 K. Lalhmingliana, " Taitea tel lovin," *El-Bethel Magazine*, 1/3 (June 1990): 2-8; K. Lalhmingliana, *El- Bethel Camp Sermon* ..., 90-100.

340 K. Lalhmingliana, "Tuihna Kang Ngailo Nun," *El-Bethel Magazine*, 1/4 (July 1990): 3-13; K. Lalhmingliana, *El- Bethel Camp Sermon* ..., 62-79.

341 K. Lalhmingliana, "Thlamuanna duh lo nun," *El-Bethel Magazine*, 1/6 (September 1990): 2-7; K. Lalhmingliana, *El- Bethel Camp Sermon* ..., 120-130.

342 K. Lalhmingliana, "Kros Hmelma ,"*El-Bethel Magazine*, 1/7, (October 1990): 2-6; K. Lalhmingliana, *El- Bethel Camp Sermon* ..., 140-147.

343 K. Lalhmingliana, "Puan In zauh ," *El-Bethel Magazine*,1/8, (November 1990): 2-8; K. Lalhmingliana, *El- Bethel Camp Sermon* ..., 80-89.

344 K. Lalhmingliana, "Remna Lal," *El-Bethel Magazine*, 1/9, (December 1990): 2-7; K. Lalhmingliana, *El- Bethel Camp Sermon* ..., 198-207.

345 K. Lalhmingliana, "Mitinin an Chhiara chu," *El-Bethel Magazine*, 2/11, (February 1991): 2-11; K. Lalhmingliana, *El- Bethel Camp Sermon* ..., 8- 24.

346 K. Lalhmingliana, "Kraws Fate Kalkawng," *El-Bethel Magazine*, 2/12, (March & April 1991): 2-9; K. Lalhmingliana, *El- Bethel Camp Sermon* ..., 157-167.

11. The Christian Life: Two Ways to Ruin *(Kristian Nun: Boralna Chihnih).* Genesis 19:15-17.[347]
12. Cross, the Powerlessness of God *(Kros Pathian Thiltihtheihlohna).* I Corinthians 1:18-18.[348]
13. The Great Banquet of God (*Pathian Ruai Ropui).* Revelation 19:17-18, Matthew 28:8-10. John 6:48-58, Luke22:19-20, I Corinthians 11:26.[349]
14. Holy Spirit the giver of Life (*Tinungtu Thlarau Thianghlim*). John 6:63.[350]
15. The aim of the Pentecost Spirit *(Penticost Thlarau Thiltum*). John 20:21-23.[351]
16. The Captive life (*Saltang nun*). Psalm 137:1-6, Colossians 3:15.[352]
17. Thy Kingdom come (*I Ram lo Thleng Rawh se*). Matthew 6:9-14.[353]
18. The Second Coming (*A Lokal lehna*). Luke 21:34-36.[354]

---

347 K. Lalhmingliana, "Kristian Nun: Boralna Chihnih," *El-Bethel Magazine*, 2/13, (May 1991): 2-6; K. Lalhmingliana, *El-Bethel Camp Sermon* ..., 131-139.

348 K. Lalhmingliana, "Kros Pathian Thiltihtheihlohna," *El-Bethel Magazine*, 2/15, (July 1991): 2-7; K. Lalhmingliana, *El- Bethel Camp Sermon* ..., 148-156.

349 K. Lalhmingliana, "Pathian Ruai Ropui," *El-Bethel Magazine*, 2/16, (August 1991); 4-10; K. Lalhmingliana, *El- Bethel Camp Sermon* ..., 187-197.

350 K. Lalhmingliana, " Tinungtu Thlarau Thianghlim," *El-Bethel Magazine*, 2/17, (September 1991): 2-7; K. Lalhmingliana, *El- Bethel Camp Sermon* ..., 25-43.

351 K. Lalhmingliana, "Penticost Thlarau Thiltum," *El-Bethel Magazine*, 2/18, (October 1991): 2-8.

352 K. Lalhmingliana, "Saltang nun," *El-Bethel Magazine*, 2/19, (November 1991): 1-5; K. Lalhmingliana, *El- Bethel Camp Sermon* ..., 111-119. Zoram Harhna Ropui - El-Bethel, Volume II (unpublished).

353 K. Lalhmingliana, "I Ram lo Thleng Rawh se," El-Bethel Magazine, 2/19, (November 1991): 6-10; *Zoram Harhna Ropui II* (unpublished).

354 K. Lalhmingliana, "A Lokal lehna," *El-Bethel Magazine*, 2/20, (December 1991): 2-10.

19. The painful heart of the loser (*Tibotu Thinlung na*). Luke 15:1-2.[355]
20. The Holy Church like an Eagle (*Mupui ang Kohhran Thianghlim*). Deut. 32:9-13.[356]
21. Two edged Sword (*Khandaih hriam tawn*). Hebrew 4:12.[357]
22. The War of God (Pathian Indona). II Chronicles 20:12, 15, II Corinthians 10:3-6.[358]
23. Pathian Thuawih (Obedience to God). Deuteronomy 21:18-21.[359]
24. Tho ila, Bethel-ah I kal ang u (Let's rise and go to Bethel). Genesis 35:1-5, Jeremiah 17:10.[360]
25. Krista a Kan Nihna (Our Nature in Christ). Colossians1:13, 19; 2:14; 3:1, Ephesians 2:1-6.[361]
26. Rah chhuah nun (the Fruit bearing Life). Ezekiel 11:19-21, John 15:5-18.[362]
27. Jacoba Pathian (The God of Jacob). Herew 2:11-12, 21; Exodus 3:6.[363]

---

355 K. Lalhmingliana, "Tibotu Thinlung na," *El-Bethel Magazine*, 3/21, (January 1992): 2-6.

356 K. Lalhmingliana, "Mupui ang Kohhran Thianghlim," El-Bethel Magazine, 3/22,(February 1992): 2-6; *Zoram Harhna Ropui II* (unpublished).

357 K. Lalhmingliana, "Khandaih hriam tawn," *El-Bethel Magazine*, 3/23,(March 1992): 5-10; *Zoram Harhna Ropui II* (unpublished).

358 K. Lalhmingliana, "Pathian Indona," *El-Bethel Magazine*, 3/23, (March 1992): 10-14.

359 K. Lalhmingliana, "Pathian Thuawih," *El-Bethel Magazine*, 3/24, (April 1992): 6-11.

360 K. Lalhmingliana, "Tho ila, Bethel-ah I kal ang u," *El-Bethel Magazine*, 3/25, (May 1992): 2-7; K. Lalhmingliana, *El- Bethel Camp Sermon ...*, 233-242.

361 K. Lalhmingliana, "Krista a Kan Nihna," *El-Bethel Magazine*, 3/25, (May 1992): 8-12; *Zoram Harhna Ropui II* (unpublished).

362 K. Lalhmingliana, "Rah chhuah nun," *El-Bethel Magazine*, 3/26, (June1992): 2-9; *Zoram Harhna Ropui II* (unpublished).

363 K. Lalhmingliana, "Jacoba Pathian," *El-Bethel Magazine*, 3/27, (July 1992): 2-9.

28. Kraws- Pathian thiltum (Cross- the Purpose of God). Genesis 3:15.[364]
29. Abrahama Pathian (The God of Abraham). Genesis 22:1-2.[365]
30. Nang Malsawmna ni ang che (Be a blessing). Isaiah 35:3; 58:6-7; Genesis12:2.[366]
31. Inremna leh Thianghlimna (Holiness and Harmony). Hebrew 12:14.[367]
32. Thu Hmanhmawh ber (The Most Urgent Word). Matthew 28:18-20.[368]
33. Jakoba Khualzin Kawng (The Pilgrims of Jacob). Genesis 47:9.[369]
34. Chhiahhlawh College (The College of Servants). Isaiah 52:13-14.[370]
35. Baptism. Mark 16:15-16.[371]
36. Thlarau Thianghlim Pawl Tharna (The Fresh fellowship of the Holy Spirit). Ephesians 2:1-6, Colossians 1:19-22, I Corinthians 6:9-11.[372]
37. Thlarau Rah (The Fruit of the Spirit). The Song of Solomon 4:16.[373]

---

364 K. Lalhmingliana, "Kraws-Pathian thiltum," *El-Bethel Magazine*, 3/28, (August 1992): 2-8.

365 K. Lalhmingliana, "Abrahama Pathian," *El-Bethel Magazine*, 3/29, (September 1992): 2-8; K. Lalhmingliana, *El-Bethel* Camp Sermon ..., 225-232.

366 K. Lalhmingliana"Nang Malsawmna ni ang che," *El-Bethel Magazine*, 4/31, (November 1992): 2-8.

367 K. Lalhmingliana, "Inremna leh Thianghlimna," *El-Bethel Magazine*, 4/32, (December 1992): 2-10.

368 K. Lalhmingliana, "Thu Hmanhmawh ber," *El-Bethel Magazine*, 4/33, (January 1993): 2-8; K. Lalhmingliana, *El-Bethel Camp Sermon ...*, 215-224.

369 K. Lalhmingliana, "Jakoba Khualzin Kawng," *El-Bethel Magazine*,4/34, (February 1993): 2-12; *Zoram Harhna Ropui II*. (unpublished).

370 K. Lalhmingliana, "Chhiahhlawh College," *El-Bethel Magazine*, 4/35, (March 1993): 2-10.

371 K. Lalhmingliana, "Baptisma," *El-Bethel Magazine*, 4/36, (April 1993): 2-9.

372 K. Lalhmingliana, "Thlarau Thianghlim Pawl Tharna," *El-Bethel Magazine*, 4/37, (May 1993): 2-6; *Zoram Harhna Ropui II* (unpublished).

373 K. Lalhmingliana, "Thlarau Rah," *El-Bethel Magazine*, 4/38, (June 1993): 2-8.

38. Kristian Chhungkua (Christian Family). Ephesians 5:33; I Corinthians 7:3, 5.[374]
39. Kraws- Pangpar Rimtui (Cross- the Aroma of the Flower). I Corinthians 1:18-19.[375]
40. Thuruk Enkawl tu (The Custodian of the Secret Word). I Corinthians 4:1-2, I John2:15, James 4:4.[376]
41. Mihring Mantu (Fisher of Men). Luke 5:8-10, Matthew 16:13-15, Mark1:16.[377]
42. Pathian Hmangaihna (The Love of God). John 3:16, 17, 14:21, I John 3:16-18, Philemon 17-19.[378]
43. Zawlnei Putar (The Old Prophet). Isaiah 30:21.[379]
44. Lei Hringnun piah ram (The Life beyond). Romans 12:1-2.[380]
45. New Jerusalem: Revelation Chapter 7, 21, 22.[381]
46. Kros Thisen Remna (The Blood of Cross for Reconciliation). Leviticus 7:1.[382]
47. Moriah Tlangah (On the Mount of Moreh). Genesis 22:1-2[383]
48. The Cross. I Corinthians 1:18.[384]

---

374 K. Lalhmingliana, "Kristian Chhungkua," *El-Bethel Magazine*, 4/39, (July 1993): 2-9; *Zoram Harhna Ropui II* (unpublished).

375 K. Lalhmingliana, "Kraws-Pangpar Rimtui," *El-Bethel Magazine*, 4/40, (August 1993): 2-5.

376 K. Lalhmingliana, "Thuruk Enkawl tu," *El-Bethel Magazine*, 5/41, (September 1993): 2-8; *Zoram Harhna Ropui II* (unpublished).

377 K. Lalhmingliana, "Mihring Mantu," *El-Bethel Magazine*, 5/42, (October 1993): 2-8.

378 K. Lalhmingliana, "Pathian Hmangaihna," *El-Bethel Magazine*, 5/43, (November 1993): 2-7.

379 K. Lalhmingliana, "Zawlnei Putar," *El-Bethel Magazine*, 5/44, (December1993): 2-8.

380 K. Lalhmingliana, "Lei Hringnun piah ram," *El-Bethel Magazine*, 5/45, (January 1994): 2 10.

381 K. Lalhmingliana, "Jerusalem Thar," *El-Bethel Magazine*, 5/46, (February 1994): 2-8.

382 K. Lalhmingliana, "Kros Thisen Remna," *El-Bethel Magazine*, 5/47, (March 1994): 2-7.

383 K. Lalhmingliana, "Moriah Tlangah," *El-Bethel Magazine*, 5/48, (April 1994): 2-8.

384 K. Lalhmingliana, "Kraws," *El-Bethel Magazine*, 5/49, (May 1994): 2-11.

49. Krista Thuhretu Rinawm (the Faithful Witnesses of Christ). I Corinthians 4:1-2, I John 2:15, James 4: 4.[385]
50. Saruak Nun (The Naked Life). Genesis 2:25.[386]
51. I Tihduhdah Isua (I Am Jesus Whom You Persecuted). Acts 9:3-6.[387]
52. Lalpaa Lawmna (Rejoicing in the Lord). Habakkuk 3:17-18.[388]
53. Thuchah Hnuhnung (The Last Will). Matthew 28:19-20.[389]
54. Dan leh Khawngaihna (Law and Grace). Romans 10:5, Galatians 3:24.[390]
55. Thih Thlamuanna (Peace In Death). Hebrew 9:27.[391]
56. The High Court of Calvary. Isaiah 53:6.[392]
57. Lalpa Siam Khawpui Thar (The New Created City of Lord). Revelation 21:1-4.[393]
58. Hnehna nun thuruk leh a Panna Kalkawng (the Secret and the Path to the Victorious Life).[394]
59. Tum Tlatna (Concrete Determination). Daniel 1:18.[395]

---

385 K. Lalhmingliana, "Krista Thuhretu Rinawm," *El-Bethel Magazine*, 5/50, (June 1994): 2-9.

386 K. Lalhmingliana, "Saruak Nun," *El-Bethel Magazine*, 6/51, (July 1994): 2-7; *Zoram Harhna Ropui II* (unpublished).

387 K. Lalhmingliana, "I Tihduhdah Isua," *El-Bethel Magazine*, 6/52, (August 1994): 2-8.

388 K. Lalhmingliana, "Lalpaa Lawmna," *El-Bethel Magazine*, 6/53, (September 1994): 2-8; *Zoram Harhna Ropui II* (unpublished).

389 K. Lalhmingliana, "Thuchah Hnuhnung," *El-Bethel Magazine*, 6/54, (October 1994): 2-8.

390 K. Lalhmingliana, "Dan leh Khawngaihna," *El-Bethel Magazine*, 6/55, (November 1994): 2-8; *Zoram Harhna Ropui II* (unpublished).

391 K. Lalhmingliana, "Thih Thlamuanna," *El-Bethel Magazine*, 6/56, (December 1994): 2-6.

392 K. Lalhmingliana, "Kalvari High Court," *El-Bethel Magazine*, 6/57, (January 1995): 2-7. *Zoram Harhna Ropui II* (unpublished).

393 K. Lalhmingliana, "Lalpa Siam Khawpui Thar," *El-Bethel Magazine*, 6/58, (February 1995): 2-9.

394 K. Lalhmingliana, "Hnehna nun thuruk leh a Panna Kalkawng," *El-Bethel Magazine*, 6/59, (March 1995): 2-7.

395 K. Lalhmingliana, "Tum Tlatna," *El-Bethel Magazine*, 6/60,(April 1995): 2-8; Zoram Harhna Ropui II (unpublished).

60. Minhriat reng nan hei hi ti thin rawh u (Do this in Remembrance of me). I Corinthians 11: 23-26.[396]
61. In dam tlang em? (Are you doing all Right?). Ezekiel 39:18; 47: 9-10.[397]
62. Thlarau Chawlhna Isua (Jesus: the Resting Place of the Soul). Matthew 11:28-30.[398]
63. Thlarau Thianghlim a lo thlenin (When the Holy Spirit Arrives). Ezekiel 11:19-21.[399]
64. Pathian Thuruk inthup Puan chhuahna (The Proclamation of the Secret Word of God). Hebrew 1:1-2.[400]
65. Zanriah Hnuhnung (The Last Supper). Luke 22:9-12.[401]
66. Damlai Tuipui Fawn Piah Lamah (Beyond the Troubled Sea of Life). Psalm 42:7.[402]
67. Retheite Lalpa (The Lord of the Poor). Psalm 116:15, Exodus 22:22-27, Psalm 82:3-4.[403]
68. Ral leh mai thin Lei Hring Nun (the Ever Vanishing Life of the World). Job 14:1-2; II Corinthians 6: 2.[404]
69. Tuinung Lui (The Living Water). Ezekiel 47: 8-11.[405]

---

396 K. Lalhmingliana, "Minhriat reng nan hei hi ti thin rawh u," *El-Bethel Magazine*, 6/60, (April 1995): 14-17.

397 K. Lalhmingliana, "In dam tlang em?," El-Bethel Magazine, 7/61, (May1995): 2-7; Zoram Harhna Ropui II (unpublished).

398 K. Lalhmingliana, "Thlarau Chawlhna Isua," *El-Bethel Magazine*, 7/62, (June 1995): 2-8.

399 K. Lalhmingliana, "Thlarau Thianghlim a lo thlenin," *El-Bethel Magazine*, 7/63, (July 1995): 2-9.

400 K. Lalhmingliana, "Pathian Thuruk inthup Puan chhuahna," *El-Bethel Magazine*, 7/65, (September 1995): 2-7; *Zoram Harhna Ropui II* (unpublished).

401 K. Lalhmingliana, "Zanriah Hnuhnung," *El-Bethel Magazine*, 7/66, (October 1995): 2-6.

402 K. Lalhmingliana, "Damlai Tuipui Fawn Piah Lamah," *El-Bethel Magazine*, 7/67, (November & December 1995): 2-7.

403 K. Lalhmingliana, "Retheite Lalpa," *El-Bethel Magazine*, 7/68, (January 1996): 2-4.

404 K. Lalhmingliana, "Ral leh mai thin Lei Hring Nun," *El-Bethel Magazine*, 7/69, (February 1996): 2-8; *Zoram Harhna Ropui II* (unpublished).

405 K. Lalhmingliana, "Tuinung Lui," *El-Bethel Magazine*, 7/70, (March 1996): 2-7.

70. Counselling Kohhran (Counselling Church).[406]

His styles of composition of the *themes* are attractive, unusual, sound negative and strange to the conventional Christian preaching but by hearing and seeing his perspectives it gives new idea and understanding, this is the peculiarity to others. Eg:

1. The Life that Negates Comforts. Psalm 77:1-4, Matthew 7:42.[407]
2. Enemy of the Cross. Philippians 3:17-20.[408]
3. Cross, the Powerlessness of God. I Corinthians 1:18-18.[409]
4. The painful heart of the loser. Luke 15:1-2.[410]
5. The College of Servants. Isaiah 52:13-14.[411]
6. Cross- the Aroma of the Flower. I Corinthians 1:18-19.[412]
7. The Naked Life. Genesis 2:25.[413]
8. Peace in Death. Hebrew 9:27.[414]

Regarding selection of the *texts* for his preaching he chose the theme first and to meet the theme then, appropriate texts are selected from the Biblical verses. Since his main aim and motto was to revive the people to be able to help the sinners. This was clearly seen in his sermons. In all the sermons proper and systematic exposition of the texts was not seen in his sermons. Most of the texts are used for illustrations.

---

406 K. Lalhmingliana, "Counselling Kohhran," *El-Bethel Magazine*, 2/14, (June 1991): 4-14; K. Lalhmingliana, *El- Bethel Camp Sermon* ..., 44-61.

407 "Thlamuanna duh lo nun," *El-Bethel Magazine* I/6 (September, 1990): 2; K. Lalhmingliana, *El- Bethel Camp Sermon* ..., 120-130.

408 "Kros Hmelma," *El-Bethel Magazine* I/7 (October, 1990): 2; K. Lalhmingliana, *El-Bethel Camp Sermon* ..., 140-147.

409 "Kros Pathian Thiltihtheihlohna," *El-Bethel Magazine* 2/15 (July, 1991), 2; K. Lalhmingliana, *El-Bethel Camp Sermon* ..., 148-156.

410 "Tibotu Thinlung na," *El-Bethel Magazine* 2/21 (January, 1992): 2.

411 "Chhiahhlawh College," *El-Bethel Magazine* 3/35 (March, 1993): 2.

412 "Kraws- Pangpar Rimtui," *El-Bethel Magazine* 4/40 (August, 1993): 2.

413 "Saruak Nun," *El-Bethel Magazine* 5/51 (July, 1994): 2.

414 "Thih Thlamuanna," *El-Bethel Magazine* 5/56 (December, 1994): 2.

1.3. Classifications of the Sermons

A survey of his indigenous preaching shows very clearly that he preached a little more from the New Testament (NT) than the Old Testament (OT). He preached 26 sermons out of seventy sermons choosing the texts only from the OT,[415] but he also preached 31 sermons using texts from the NT.[416] He preached only five sermons choosing the texts together from the Old and New Testaments.[417] We can say that his preaching from both the OT and NT is balanced. Especially out of 26 sermons from the book of the OT he preached 11 sermons from the prophets,[418] out of eleven sermons, six are preached from the Book of Isaiah; [419] it seems that Isaiah was his favourite text in the OT. He also preached three sermons from the Book of Ezekiel.[420]

In the NT, the Gospel of Luke seems to be his favourite gospel and he preached five sermons from Luke,[421] and four sermons from Matthew,[422] Three from John[423] and only one sermon from Mark.[424] Most of the sermons have a single text, out of 70 sermons, 44 have

---

415 From only Old Testament serial numbers, 2, 3, 4, 7, 8, 10, 11, 20, 23, 24, 28, 29, 30, 34, 37, 43, 46, 47, 50, 52, 56, 59, 61, 63, 66, 67, 69 are preached with out using a texts from the New Testament, they are 27 sermons, see Appendix No. 4.

416 From only New Testament he preaches serial number, 1, 6, 12, 13, 14, 15, 17, 18, 19, 21, 25, 31, 32, 35, 36, 39, 40, 41, 42, 44, 45, 48, 49, 51, 53, 54, 55, 60, 62, 64, 65 with out using the Text from The Old Testament, they are 31 sermons.

417 Serial number 5, 9, 26, 27, and 68.

418 The following serial Numbers are preached from the Book of Prophets 2, 4, 7, 24, 34, 43, 52, 56, 59, 61, 63, 69 they are 12 sermons.

419 From Isaiah the following serial numbers are preached: 4, 7, 8, 34, 43, 56 they are six sermons.

420 From Ezekiel the following serial numbers are preached: 61, 63, 69 they are three sermons.

421 From Luke the following serial number: 1. 18. 19, 41, 65 are preached they are five sermons.

422 From Mathew serial number 17, 32, 53, 62 are preached they are four sermons.

423 From John, serial number 14, 15, 42 are preached they are three sermons.

424 Serial number 35 is the only sermon from the Gospel of St. Mark.

single texts[425] and only 24 sermons have double texts and two sermons are text less.[426] From the OT, 24 books are not touched as a text of the sermon,[427] and from the NT, 10 books are not used as text of the sermon,[428] all of them are Epistles.

The nature of the hearers was taken into consideration. But their political and economic situation was not given sufficient attention. He was worried about and spoke against social problems, alcoholism, sustenance of the poor, caring of drug abusers, commercial sex workers, problems in Christian family and he tended to preach mostly on spiritual themes. In his preaching the exposition of the biblical text takes place according to the context. That K. Hminga did not give sufficient attention to the exegesis of the text and thereby neglected the interpretative situation can be clearly seen in the analysis of some sermons in this study.

2. Themes of the Sermons and Biblical References in the Tanhril Camp

At the Tanhril Camp organized by the Chanmari and Dawrpui Vengthar Pastorate he preached twelve (12) sermons in each Camp. The following table contains the order of sermons with the Biblical References preached in the Tanhril Camp.[429]

425 Serial number 2, 4, 6, 7, 8, 10, 11, 12, 14, 15, 17, 18, 19, 20, 23, 28, 29, 31, 32, 33, 34, 35, 37, 39, 43, 44, 46, 47, 48, 50, 51, 52, 53, 55, 56, 57, 59, 60, 62, 63, 64, 65, 66, and 69 are having only a single Text in the sermon.

426 Serial Number 58 & 70.

427 The Book of Numbers, Joshua, Judges, Ruth, I Samuel, I & II Kings, I Chronicles, Ezra, Nehemiah, Esther, Ecclesiastes, Lamentations, Hosea, Joel, Amos, Obadiah, Jonah, Micah, Nahum, Zephaniah, Haggai, Zachariah and Malachi.

428 The book of I & II Thessalonians, I &II Timothy, Titus, I & II Peter, II & III John and Jude.

429 Pi. Chuhveli attends the ministers camp on 15th-18th.1.1990 and recorded the Time, sermon, themes, Biblical References in her camp Note Book (unpublished).

Table: Showing Date, Time, Themes of the Sermons and Biblical references of El-Bethel Camp at Tanhril

Date	Time	Theme	Biblical References
15. 1.1990	3-4PM	The life of Prayer	Joshua.10:21, Joel.1:13, 2:17
	5:30-6:30	Humility: The Gospel that Reaches Sinners	Luke 5:29-30, 10:30-35, 19:5-7
16.1.1990	6 -7:00AM	The Painful Heart of the Loser	Luke. 15:1-32, Jeremiah 8:4
	10:30-11:30AM	The Life that Negates Comfort	Matthew 27:42, Psalm 77:1-10.
	5:30-6:30 PM	The Love of God	John 3:16-17, I John 3:16-17
17.1.1990	6 -7:00AM	Fishers of Men	Mark. 1:16, Luke5:4, Matthew16: 13.
	10:30-11:30AM	The Holy Church like an Eagle	Deut.32:9-13.
18.1.1990	6 -7:00AM	Our Nature in Him	Ephesians 2:1-6, Colossians1:13, 19-20, 2:14,3:1
	10:30-11:30AM	The Great Banquet of God	Revelation19:17-18, Luke 22:19 Matthew22:8, John 6:48.
	2-3:00 PM	Rejoice in the Lord	Habakkuk 3:17-18
	5:30-6:30, PM	The Living River	Ezekiel 47:6-12.
19.1.1990	6:00-8:00AM	Without the Lad	Genesis44:30ff, Proverb24:11ff, 22:6.

3. Analysis of the Sermons

Out of the seventy sermons of K. Lalhmingliana the following five sermons are selected for analysis because of their variation in message, content, application, and use of illustrations. It is difficult to have a standard criterion for analysis of the sermons in the indigenous revival preaching that usually centre on conversion and renewal.[430] The objective of the preaching is clear, it is achieved and it revives the people, but regarding the structure, contents and exposition like other various types of sermons it is difficult to have a standard principle.

3.1. Theme: Humility: The Gospel that Reaches Sinners

Biblical text: Luke 5: 29-32; 10:30-35; 19: 5-7.

3.1.1. Information about the Sermon

The sermon has been taken from *El-Bethel Magazine*, Vol. I, No. I, April 1990, 9-12, and the book of *El- Bethel Camp Sermon*, Vol. I page 1-7. He preached on 15.1.1990, 5:30-6:30 PM in the Camp organized by the Chanmari and Dawrpui Vengthar Pastorate.[431] This sermon is the main motto of the team and was preached in each camp, and seems to have been preached more than 270 times in the years 1987-2004.[432]

3.1.2. Formal Elements of Sermon

a. The Beginning

The preacher began his sermon by reading the Biblical text, and he introduced the theme as the main theme of the El-Bethel Evangelical Team, stating that all the preaching of the El-Bethel team focuses towards the sinners. For the introduction of the sermon he shared his experiences:

---

430 Timothy P. Weber, "Revivals," *Concise Encyclopaedia of Preaching*, edited by William H. Willimon and Richard Lischer (Louisville: Westminster John Knox Press, 1995): 406-409.

431 Pi. Chuhveli camp Note Book (unpublished).

432 Thanchhunga, Interviewed on 28.4.2006 at his residence.

> I accepted Jesus as My Lord and saviour on Feb. 1962 but without the fellowship of the Holy Spirit, I continued my ministry. Because of my devotion to of the church, I was very cruel to the drug addicts and drunkards and tormented them badly; they were very afraid of me and they could not even come near my house. I was proud of doing such duties; even some friends told me that they hated these drunkards and mischief makers. But on 18 April, 1978 the Holy Spirit came to me and changed my life. One day the Holy Spirit used John 5 in which Jesus encountered the paralyzed man who had been ill for 38 years. I felt that I was also with them, when I heard that Jesus was asking, "Do you want to be made well?" If he said, "Yes, I want to be made well," there would be no effect on me, but his answer was very shameful to me, saying that, " Sir, I have no one to put me into the pool when the water is stirred up; and while I am making my way, someone else steps down ahead of me." When I heard his answer, I really felt pained that I was the one who did not help and avoided my duty; I was really surprised, ashamed, humiliated and had nothing to say to God I saw myself and felt guilty. My heart was full of pain, and then I prayed to God by telling my commitment that, "God, from now onward make me as a man of help for those who are helpless." From that day onwards my life was really changed and many helpless people came to my house and I helped them as much as possible. This was my turning point toward God's ministry.[433]

He also used the adulterous woman who was brought to Jesus to know his view:

> I saw myself as among the people ready to stone the woman. When Jesus asked the people to start stoning if they are sinless, all of them secretly moved away. I was left alone with the woman and stood quietly with a stone. My shame was added, when Jesus proclaimed, "Woman, where are

433 *El-Bethel Camp Sermon…*, 2-3.

> they? Has no one condemned you?" She said, "No one, sir." And Jesus said, "Neither do I condemn you." (NRSV) The stone was very disturbing and really shameful to me; I was surprised, shocked, and really regretted. I realized that I was also a sinner but still standing to kill the woman. That really changed my mind toward the sinners.[434]

The above two experiences were used for the clarification of the introduction of his sermon. Through these examples he explains that he was the one who tortured, hated the sinners, drug addicts, alcoholics and drove them away instead of helping and supporting these people. And he learned that the messages what he has preached did not reach the sinners. Instead of reaching them he treated them badly and drove them away. But from that day of apprehension, many drunkards, drug addicts and alcoholics came to his house, even in the midnight. Some would vomit on the floor and he used to clean them. No one was afraid of him like the previous life. Then he continued to say that from that day onward his ministry to these people became a glorious job. The above statement occupies nearly one third of the sermon.

b. The Middle

The development of the sermon took place under three points. Firstly, helping and supporting, the sinners is a glorious job and the will of God. Second, the conventional ministry of the church is not adequate. Third, he mentioned the need of the baptism of the Holy Spirit for positive attitude toward the sinners and to take responsibility to bring them back to Christ.

The discussion of the theme took place in the form of illustrations and uses the text of Luke 19:5-7 (encounter of Zacchaeus and Jesus) by taking as an illustration of the love of Jesus to the sinners. And he states that, "*the people who grumble and say, "He has gone to be the guest of one who is a sinner" (NRSV) are the pious and religious people who think that they are good, but do not bother and love the sinners.*" In the same manner, he used the text Lk.10:30-35 that the

---

434 *El-Bethel Magazine* 1/I (April, 1990): 9-12; K. Lalhmingliana, *El-Bethel Camp Sermon...*, 3.

Priest and Levite did not care for the helpless person on the road to Jericho. But the humble Samaritan nursed and put him on the donkey while he walked by foot. Through these illustrations the preacher examines the heart of the people, whether their ministry reaches the life of sinners: 'many people are facing robbers in their life between the road of heavenly Jerusalem and Jericho. The gospel preachers in today's world did not reach what they have to reach. This is wrong; most of the people do not open their heart to the sinners but only to the good and rich people' (p. 5). He appeals the people to examine what kind of gospel they have; whether they are the ones with stones to kill the sinners or the one who left the helpless alone. He says "*the emergent need of the message in society is **the Gospel that reaches the sinners;** this can be implemented only through **humility**"* (p. 5). For this he used one illustration of one doctor who receives a fresh baptism of the Holy Spirit, and who was really changed and compassionate to the poor and alcoholics. He blamed the present ministry of the churches that does not reach the sinners but only the good people. And he requested the people to pray to God for forgiveness of their mistake that their gospel never reached the sinners. And he also taught them what to say in their prayer "*Teach me to love your beloved with whom you have dinner (Jesus took dinner with the sinners), give me your tender heart to love and care your beloved*" (p. 5). The above illustrations occupy nearly two thirds of the texts in the sermon.

c. The End

The sermon came to an end by summarizing the story that the Samaritan put the helpless patient on the donkey, and then he himself walked by foot. Likewise he requests the audience to humble themselves to care for the weak and sinners. He also quotes the word of Jesus, "For the Son of Man came to seek out and to save the lost, (NRSV) Lk.19:10." And he requested the people to confess and repent for the baptism of the Holy Spirit. Therefore the love of God towards sinners will dwell in them and their main concern will turn toward the sinners, then all the sinners will receive the Gospel. In the conclusion he identifies himself directly with the campers when he says: "*May God Bless his Holy Word for us all.*"[435]

3.1.3. Appraisal of the Sermon

The preacher had one interest and that was that the ministry of the church should be focused mainly on the sinners, and he blamed the conventional ministry of the churches of not meeting the needs of the sinners. He allegorized the Priest and Levites as representing the church leaders who neglected the ministry towards the sinners. For this he blamed his previous ministry in the church but after he received Spiritual Baptism he became a new man and was able to direct his ministry towards the sinners.

The structure of the sermon shows continuity;[436] at the same time it moved toward a climax.[437] For this the use of illustrations helped the preacher, and produced long lasting impression[438] on its hearers.[439]

The sermon raises some important homiletical issues. The preacher assumes that his hearers are only nominal Christians, and claimed himself as the one who received the baptism of the Holy Spirit while all the campers have not yet received.[440] Campers need to receive the baptism of the Holy Spirit without which the ministerial activity was worthless.

Actually due to the existing ministries of the church he was invited to speak to the churches. These ministries were carried out because of the guidance of the Holy Spirit, so it is not safe to blame the conventional ministries were carried out with out the presence of the Holy Spirit. But such concern of the sinners was the obligation and need of the church.

---

435 *El-Bethel Magazine* 1/I (April, 1990): 12; K. Lalhmingliana, *El-Bethel Camp Sermon…*, 7.

436 Ralph G. Turnbull, ed., *Baker's Hand Book of Practical Theology* (Michigan: Baker Book House, 1967), 73.

437 Ibid.

438 Ibid.

439 When interview was conducted, many respondents, interviewee can pin point the theme and messages of the El-bethel preaching, when they were asked.

440 Some are Pastors, Elders, and volunteer workers in the churches (ministers).

As W. Steward says, "preaching is a responsible spiritual ministry which a man may dare to discharge only when he has sincerely and humbly 'listened' for the Word of God in study of the scripture with prayer."[441] K. Hminga mainly preached from his study and experiences. He presented himself as an example in caring and loving and relating to the sinners: '*before I received the baptism of the Holy Spirit..., I used to torture ..., they were afraid of me...,* (p. 1) *I drove them away..., I feel ashamed ..., Make me your servant...,* (p. 2) *I realized ..., they come to my house...,* (p. 3) *I used to clean...., I care..., my ministry...,* (p. 4).

The flow of the sermon is attractive but there is practically no exegesis of the Biblical text in the sermon. K. Hminga does not intend to preach from the texts as he simply introduces it. Biblical references were not used appropriately; the first text was not mentioned in the sermon body again. He just used the texts for illustrations. The speaker was led by the theme not by the texts. From this we can identify that his type is Topical sermon, 'in which the entire treatment of the sermon depends upon the topic.'[442]

He was allegorizing the hurt person and the sinners in the similar status but it is difficult to accept. There may be likeness but the wounded person and the poor, addicts, alcoholics, CSW are different. He stated that "*currently there are many people who faced robbers between Jericho and heavenly Jerusalem*" (p. 5). Here he allegorizes robbers with, drugs, alcohol, sex, poverty. Allegorizing human and material is difficult to accept. He needed to be careful in using the illustrations as Dr. G. Isaiah cautioned the preacher in using illustrations in relation to the lives of the people who are hearing the preaching.[443]

Regarding the voice and articulation, it can be seen through the Video and audio recording,[444] the voice was soft, appealing and very interesting and natural like Spurgeon, Moody, Finney and

441 William Steward, *The Nature and Calling of The Church ...,* 161.

442 Ralph G. Turnbull, ed., *Baker's Hand Book ...,* 58.

443 G. Isaiah, *Preach the Word: The Basics of Homiletics* (Tiruvalla: Christa Sahitya Samithi, 2004), 119.

444 Audio recording of the sermon of K. Lalhmingliana. n.d.

Whitefield;[445] it was related to his fluent in articulation. Sharing his practical experiences made him confident and mastered the sermon since it was often preached in the Gospel Camps.

The sermon was concluded by mixing *summarization* and *making application method* of conclusion.[446] It was 'appropriate for the occasion, audience and the sermon.'[447] The sermon took 27 minutes.

3.2. Theme: The Painful Heart of the Loser

Biblical Reference: Luke 15:1-32.

3.2.1. Information about the Sermon

The sermon has been taken from *El-Bethel Magazine*, Vol. II, No. 21, January 1992, 2-6, and the book of *El- Bethel Camp Sermon*, Vol. I page 225-232. He preached on 16.1.1990, 6-7 PM in the Camp organized by the Chanmari and Dawrpui Vengthar Pastorate.[448] It was also preached and repeated many times in El-Bethel Camp, and seems to be preached more than 100 times in the year 1987-2004.[449]

3.2.2. Formal Elements of Sermon

a. The Beginning

The preacher began his sermon by reading the Biblical text, and introduced the theme of the Sermon "We shall call **the painful heart of the loser** as our theme" (p. 225). He mentioned that there are three types of lost: the lost Sheep, the lost Coin and the Prodigal Son. He stated that many people tax collectors, sinners came to Jesus. Meanwhile the good people like Pharisees, Scribes were annoyed,[450]

---

445 Lloyd M. Perry and John R. Strubhar, *Evangelistic Preaching* (Chicago: Moody Press, 1979), 125.

446 G. Isaiah, *Preach the Word: ...*, 123.

447 Ibid., 124.

448 Pi. Chuhveli camp Note Book (unpublished).

449 K. Hawla Interviewed on 28.4. 2006 at his residence.

450 (NRSV). Then Levi gave a great banquet for him in his house; and there was a large crowd of tax collectors and others sitting at the table with them. The Pharisees and their scribes were complaining to his disciples, saying, "Why do

and then Jesus explained the purpose of His coming by using the parable of the lost Sheep, that not for the 99 good people but for the one who is lost. He also explained through the lost Coin that the owner does no seek the nine coins but the lost one. The nine coins are not in the heart of the owner but the lost coin, when it was found, the owner rejoiced and told the neighbours. Even with the prodigal son, it was not the matter of the son but the painful heart of the father. While the son was still on the way the father did not hang around his arrival, rather he ran, tenderly embraced, and kissed him, "this prospect resulted the theme of the sermon."[451] "*Without the sinners, God cannot be quiet and happy rather waiting the return of the sinners to him, his heart is painful due to the sinners,*" Here the preacher stated that "*the heart of God is occupied by the sinners, they were significant to Him.*"(p. 225).

b. The Middle

The development of the sermon took place in three ways. First the love of God is extreme and incomparable. For this he used the illustration of the incarnate life of Jesus Christ. Second, the heart of God is pained and suffers in the suffering of the people. Here he quoted Jeremiah 8: 7,[452] 18-20.[453] He illustrated the churches, society, some leaders and family members distrust and reject the sinners; and he stated that the mature Christians are not worried for the lives of others and offer more prayer for self. Third is qualification

---

you eat and drink with tax collectors and sinners?" Jesus answered, "Those who are well have no need of a physician, but those who are sick; I have come to call not the righteous but sinners to repentance." Lk. 5:29-32.

451 K. Lalhmingliana, *El- Bethel Camp Sermon* ..., 226.

452 Even the stork in the heavens, knows its times; and the turtledove, swallow, and crane observe the time of their coming; but my people do not know the ordinance of the LORD.

453 (NRSV).My joy is gone, grief is upon me, and my heart is sick. Hark, the cry of my poor people from far and wide in the land: "Is the LORD not in Zion? Is her King not in her?"("Why have they provoked me to anger with their images, with their foreign idols?") "The harvest is past, the summer is ended, and we are not saved." For the hurt of my poor people I am hurt, I mourn, and dismay has taken hold of me. Is there no balm in Gilead? Is there no physician there? Why then has the health of my poor people not been restored?

for servant minister. For this the call of God told him two things: 1. How worthy are the sinners in the heart of God? (229), he was longing to know, "how profound a place do the sinners occupy in the heart of God?"[454] 2. To qualify for the servant of God (229). He stated that ministry to God is not from the sonship but from servant hood and humility. Such humility was the nature of God and he emptied himself to become a servant. He stated that qualifying to be a servant of God is not easy. He closed the middle by the word, "After only becoming a real servant, we can know the worth of sinners in the heart of God and we can only begin to love those sinners" (231).

c. The End

He appealed to the campers to return to the Lord, 'since God cannot be happy without the sinners, his heart is paining, God is eagerly waiting for our return, and let's say, "Lord I am coming, I do not know how to come, draw me near to you," He will surely embrace us. Then the seeker and the lost will meet and not only the people of heaven, but also the churches, family and society will rejoice, so let us return to him, since his heart is painful without us.' This application to return is the conclusion of the sermon. In the conclusion he identified himself directly with the campers when he said: "*May God Bless his Word for us all.*"[455]

3.2.3. Appraisal of the Sermon

The whole emphasis is related to the painful heart of the loser God and eagerly waiting the return of the sinners. He did not emphasize how worthy the 99 good people are but only stressed the single lost one. He stated that in the heart of God the single lost was more important than the 99. But this does not mean that God is not concerned with the 99. It signifies that God is not partial. He loves and cares for all. K. Hminga stressed not about the lost but the loser. This peculiar type of illustration is found throughout his sermons. He regarded that God is not pleased in the absence of the sinners. To bring them back to God is taking initiative. This was illustrated

454 K. Lalhmingliana, *El- Bethel Camp Sermon …*, 229.

455 Ibid., 232.

through the incarnation of Jesus. But still human beings are turning away from him and God's pain continues.

In this sermon, he used three illustrations from the text[456] and one from the forgiven adulterous woman and his experiences with the CSWs (p. 230-231); "*It is shameful Lord, seeking evasion to love whom you love. Am I anxious of bad reputation because of your dear ones?* The illustrations are appropriately used and serve as a vital source of power and illumination to the sermon;[457] but the interpretation is diverse from the usual interpretation.[458]

The structure is not organized accurately and there is no proper division in the point system. So it is difficult to have clear cut understanding for the audience. But the flow of the sermon helps them to carry on; here we can see the importance of theological education in relation to the structure of the sermon.

This type of preaching is topical sermon by structure. The preacher is not concerned about exegesis to the text, and it is freely developed by the preacher. But the danger is that no systematic teaching is provided through this type of sermon.[459] Exposition of the text is the need in the sermon; he is not concerning to the text but the theme and his goal of the sermon.

The preacher tried to preach from his experience. He presented himself as an example to show the difficulty to become the servant of God: *I used to think...I stopped praying for myself...I pray only for others...* (p. 229) *I pray for two things* ...(p. 229) *I used to pick up to stone...I kneel down...when I see...*(p. 230) *When I was revived... humility was my... I realized... I was unworthy... My on going prayer item...I feel a shame...* (p. 231). He drew most of his analogies from his experience. He related his experience to his preaching. To some extent it can be categorized under experiential preaching.

The language used by the preacher is simple and interesting. He was good in articulation; and it is even more obvious by listening

456 The lost Sheep, the lost Coin, and the Prodigal Son.

457 James S. Steward, *Heralds of God* (Michigan: Baker Book House, 1974), 143.

458 They are usually interpreted to show the love and forgiveness of God upon the repentant person.

459 G. Isaiah, *Preach the Word: ...*, 92.

to the audio than reading the manuscript. And it is also inclusive that he identified himself with the audiences and formulated his sentences in the form of "our" (24 times) "us, we" (28 times). It is truly inclusive not subversive. The sermon took 25 minutes,[460] and it was tolerable to the campers.

3.3. Theme: The Life that Negates Comfort

Biblical Reference: Psalm 77:1- 4, Matthew 7: 42

3.3.1. Information about the Sermon

The sermon has been taken from *El-Bethel Magazine*, Vol. I, No.6, Sept. 1990, 2-7, and the book of K. Lalhmingliana, *El- Bethel Camp Sermon*, Vol. I, p.120 -130. He preached on 16 Jan. 1990, 10:30-11:30 AM in the Camp organized by the Chanmari and Dawrpui Vengthar Pastorates.[461] It was also preached many times in El-Bethel Camp, and seems to have been preached more than 170 times in the years 1987-2004.[462]

3.3.2. Formal Elements of Sermon

a. The Beginning

The preacher began his sermon by reading the Biblical text, and introduced the theme of the Sermon "We shall call the theme, **The Life that Negates Comforts,** You might be surprised of hearing such a theme because most of you are coming for seeking peace and new life" (p.120). He continued that the life of believers begins with joy, peace, happiness and anointing of the Holy Spirit. For this he used an illustration of a dry machine in which oil is put and compared the anointing of the Holy Spirit with the machine of fresh oiling that can function accordingly. But the dry machine cannot function well without oil. So, he introduced that the inspiration of the Holy Spirit as the real need of the People. But he says:

> Now we are freshly anointed by the Holy Spirit, but this position is not the permanent. We should not expect to fill

460 *Sermon of K. Lalhmingliana*, Audio cassette.

461 Pi. Chuhveli camp Note Book (unpublished).

462 K. Hawla Interviewed on 28.4.2006 at his residence.

> us regularly rather we must make use of this life to help others, live in humility, seeking the lost and we need to pray to God to fill us again when it is over. It is not ours, but the gift of God, but we must utilise this kind of blessing regularly.[463]

This kind of utilisation should be acted through faith. He illustrates the faith of Christians by using the previous sermon in relation to the healing service that by faith they are to proclaim their healing, not after observation whether they are really healed or not. He said, "You should not suspect by observing the miraculous work of the Holy Spirit, but you should just accept and proclaim that you are healed. Now you are healed and just believe it and accept it. That is the Christian life."

b. The Middle

He explained the theme by asking, 'who are the ones who negate comfort in their life?, And he says that, "You may think that what I said is opposite in the Christian life. There is a time when we are seeking peace, but there should be a time of negating comfort in our life" (p.122). There is a time when humans should pray for blessing but there should also be a time when it is not prayed for. To explain this idea he used four illustrations from the texts.

1. The three friends of Daniel:[464] "...They are not confident whether they will be rescued or die in 'the furnace of blazing fire,'[465] but what they are confident is that they shall not deny their God. They do not want to save their life from the furnace of blazing fire; rather they prefer and are ready to die for God by negating peace for their life..." (123-124).

2. Daniel in the lion's den: "... He was faithful and prays to God by turning toward Jerusalem, then he was thrown into the Lion's den, " *it is not that let the lions' mouth be shut first before you throw me, but to be thrown first and the mouth of the lion was shut....*" (p.124)

---

463 K. Lalhmingliana, *El-Bethel Camp Sermon...*, 121.

464 Shadrach, Meshach, and Abednego Daniel 3:23. (NRSV).

465 NRSV.

3. The Life of David: In this illustration he mention that David was repeatedly run after by Saul trying to kill him; at the same time there were lots of chances for David to kill King Saul to avoid such disorderly life. *But his life was 'a life that negates comfort'* (Psalm 77:2*). If he were seeking comfort he should have killed him before but he didn't.*

4. The Suffering of Christ on the Cross: Jesus can call down more than twelve legions of angels (NRSV), to rescue him but it was not done for the sake of others. "Let us look to Calvary, where God cannot heal himself due to others. If it is for the comforts of others, they prefer to be in the point of loss, suffering and death; such is the life that the cross is pointing towards" (p.125).

After stating the illustration, he challenged the audience by raising the question such as whether they will seek comfort again in the future; whenever they are hungry, will they seek food? Will they seek comfort in the place of suffering, in the point of loss, thirst and in the point of losing faith? (p.125) He requests them to be careful if they are in such circumstances. He states "*do not expect the comfort of God in advance before something happen you, must just face it first that is the life that negates comfort.*" (p.123) Then, he summarized the faithfulness of the illustrated persons and the preacher recited the text of Psalm 77:1-4. He states:

> if God is giving you to face, to do something, just do it, do not bargain, refuse or arrange some other means, whether it is hard or horrible, sometimes it may affect our business, profession, health, we should not ask 'who did these'? In such situation, will you seek comfort? He can heal others but not himself, such is the point of the Cross which we are to achieve. (p.126)

Here, he explains that such life is the life of those who negate comfort (127). Here, he uses another illustration of a faithful girl of Romania during the time of Christian persecution. She was the only one who did not spit on the picture of Jesus Christ; rather she kissed and cleaned the dirty face with her frock. Here, the girl negates comforts and prefers death, but she was the only one who survived. Such is the life that negates comfort. Then, he quotes the word of Jesus, "for whosoever will save his life shall lose it; but whosoever shall lose his life for my sake and the gospel's, the same shall save it."[466] Then he concludes the central idea by saying, '*the most beautiful thing in the life of Jesus was not his miraculous ministry nor the beautiful glowing face in the mount of transfiguration, but the life on the cross that he cannot save himself for the sake of others this was the most beautiful incident even till today.*'

c. The End

He states that to show this beautiful nature of Calvary, God chose the church to portray such life to the world; but it is still not easy. He states, "*The nature of the Christian is too advanced; I am eagerly waiting to attain weakness, in the position where we can do nothing for our self justification. In which we will be like the lamb that does not open mouth for self justification. The nature of the lamb must be portrayed to the world; in such status there is no possibility to open mouth for self justification*" (p. 130). In such a state others will see the wonderful true nature of Jesus Christ in him/her, and Jesus will be glorified in the churches and in the life of the individual. In the conclusion he identifies himself directly with the campers when he said: "*May God Bless his Word for us all.*"[467]

3.3.3. Appraisal of the Sermon

The primary interest of the preacher is to call his listeners for a life of negating comfort. This kind of life is the life found on the Cross in which Jesus negates comfort and prefers to die for the sinners. The preacher calls upon his listeners to choose such a life, and it can be attained through the Baptism of the Holy Spirit. This kind of life refusing comforts is very rare in the life of the present Christians, but it is the need of the Christians.

To clarify his statements, he uses four illustrations (Daniel, his three friends, King David and the suffering on The Cross) from the Bible and one from the historical incident (Rumanian Girl), and one example familiar to the people (i.e., oiling Machine). All the

466 Mark 8:35, *The King James Version*, (Cambridge: Cambridge), 1769.

467 K. Lalhmingliana, *El- Bethel Camp Sermon* ..., 130.

five illustrations were relevant for the message, and made the sermon touching and 'interesting.'[468] It sounds simple[469] and was easy to understand because most of the illustrations are familiar to the people. But the illustrations were too long for a single sermon; they dominate the sermon occupying 2/3 (two thirds) of the sermon. The scholars reject this type,[470] though they are supportive to the message of the sermon.

Exposition of the text is not done; rather the texts are used for an illustration of the theme. This always happens in a Topical or Life-situational sermons.[471] This can be a disadvantage of this type of sermon. As G. Isaiah stated, "the biblical text simply becomes a pretext in the hands of the preacher for accomplishing their agenda."[472] The way he uses the text we can know what he is, James W. Cox says, "A text is the reminder of who we are, where we are going, and what we ought to be doing."[473] The texts are not properly exposed which can create confusion in Biblical interpretation.

The application part is not convincing enough "When others misinterpret and gossips about us, what will be our response? Are we the Christians who use sword to slash down the other's ear like Peter? Our efforts slashed down others' ears, but in this status, we have no feelings or desire to say our justice, justify ourselves rather for the sake of others we are ready to suffer for other..., that should be our nature."(p.129) It is not appealing enough but the main body of the sermon helps the application become meaningful for the audience.

Unlike the other sermons the "I" is not regular in this sermon; rather he includes himself directly with the audience and uses, the word "*we*" in this sermon. For example, 'we may say... (p. 120) ...*we need the Holy Spirit*.... (p. 120), *our mind*.... (p.121), God *anointed us*.... (p. 212) ... *we can do nothing* (p. 121), *Let us*.... (p. 121)...

468 W. E Sangster, *The Craft of the Sermon* (London: The Epworth Press, 1964), 207.

469 Lloyd M. Perry and John R. Strubhar, *Evangelistic Preaching* (Chicago: Moody Press, 1979), 126.

470 G. Isaiah, *Preach the Word:* ..., 119.

471 Ralph G. Turnbull, ed., *Baker's Hand Book* ..., 61.

472 G. Isaiah, *Preach the Word:* ..., 91.

473 James W. Cox, *A Guide to Biblical Preaching* (Nashville: Abingdon, 1923), 31.

we always need (p. 121*), we confess....* (p. 122), *we pray not for....* (p. 122) ... *our future* (p.125), *in this state we use to...* (p. 126), ... *our weak point* (p. 126*), we justify our self...*(p. 130), *We do not humble...*(p. 130), *we need such life...*(p.130), *our Christianity...* (130), *we are too active...*(p. 130), etc.

The preacher is fluent using appropriate words, and he is good in articulation. The language of the sermon is 'appropriate, convincing and clear.'[474] The preacher does not introduce new material in the conclusion. The sermon's duration is 25 minutes.

3.4. Theme: Fishers of Men

Biblical Reference Luke 5:8-10.[475]

3.4.1. Information about the Sermon

The sermon has been taken from *El-Bethel Magazine*, Vol. IV, No. 42, Oct. 1993, 2-8. He preached on 17.1.1990, 6-7 AM[476] in the Camp organized by the Chanmari and Dawrpui Vengthar Pastorate. It was also preached many times in El-Bethel Camp, and seems to have been preached more than 230 times in the years 1987-2004.[477]

3.4.2. Formal Elements of Sermon

a. The Beginning

The preacher began his sermon by reading the Biblical text, and introduces the theme of the Sermon "*We shall call the theme,* **Fishers of Men.**" And he continues the introduction by saying, "*Whoever is born in Spirit, their mind is full of desire to bring people to God.*" Here he includes himself by saying "*we took enormous effort to bring people to Christ, and by sponsoring and sending missionaries, and offering many offerings with unceasing prayer, but it was not effective as we expected. What is the reason? We will try to study the reason why.*" Here he concluded the introduction.

474 G. Isaiah, *Preach the Word...*, 124.

475 *El-Bethel Magazine*5/42 (October 1993): 2-8.

476 Pi. Chuhveli Note Book (unpublished).

477 K. Hawla Interviewed on 28th April, 2006 at his residence.

b. The Middle

He continues by stating the two answers of the above questions 1. To be real fishers of men one needs to catch himself. Then he questions, how can a person catch him/herself? He stated the answer; firstly '*due to the works of the Holy Spirit we realized that we are sinners, weak and unworthy in the sight of God.*' Secondly '*With the help of others God catches us.*' Here, others mean relatives, friends, colleagues. Here he states that 'catching' means revealing the weak points, failures and shortcomings of the person by friends, workmates and families. Here he stated that '*due to the work of Holy Spirit and through others God helps us to catch ourself.*' For this, he uses the illustration of Naaman who suffered from leprosy. A captive young girl said to her mistress, "If only my lord were with the prophet who is in Samaria! He would cure him of his leprosy."[478] Here, K. Hminga says that the girl was the one who exposed the undisclosed leprosy of Naaman; to him disclosing the negative weak nature of the others is to help the person realize himself. Here, K. Hminga states that '*in our spiritual life God reveals that we are sinners, and we are sorry for it and cry for repentance, but we could not understand that God uses others, to catch our self.*'

He insists on the audience that they might be criticized by others in their nature of living in negative ways. But, he states that all grumbling coming to them are sent by God to help them to recognize their real nature from the point of others. Here he uses another illustration from Matthew 16:13-16. Jesus asked his disciples, "Who do people say that the Son of Man is?" And they said, "Some say John the Baptist, but others Elijah, and still others Jeremiah or one of the prophets." He said to them, "But who do you say that I am?" Simon Peter answered, "You are the Messiah, the Son of the living God." (NRSV) His disciples had a deeper understanding than others. He uses himself as another illustration, like Jesus:

> "Who do people say that K. Hminga is?" People may say he was good preacher, dedicated. It may be true, but without knowing the closer response it is foolish to accept their comments. My wife, my children and my team members

---

478 II King 5:3 (NRSV).

> know me much deeper than others; their answers will be different. Likewise, people may admire you, since they do not see the negative side, so the comments of others is not your reality, they only see the external positive nature, but your real nature was deeply known and seen by your spouse and your family members. Your behavior in the family and your behavior outside the family are too different; you may be a good preacher but do your families acknowledge you're preaching positively? Our family members know our conduct much deeper than others. (p. 4)

Here he uses other illustrations; one from Ecclesiastes 2:15 where the composer was asking for help to catch the little foxes that ruined the vineyard,[479] and another from a local episode, he comments that these two people do not catch themselves but catch the others.[480]

He stated that, "without catching our self we blame others and preach sermons, but people also blame us in return, which shape our ministry. People may say you are drunkard, awkward, lazy, you will respond, and then hostility may begin." So, he continued by using other illustrations from his personal life that his negative, weak points that he could not know by himself were always revealed by his wife; that was really constructive and helpful for his ministry. This takes seven illustrations; some are humorous, interesting, relevant and informative. Then he closed the illustration by stating 'my wife is a real guide to catch myself.' Then he challenges the audience:

> Will you allow your wife and children to make corrections in your personal life? They will have many things to say about your negative behavior, will you accept it positively? They are the ones who know your hidden life, but that is the right way of knowing yourself. Unless you catch yourself

479 Song of Solomon 2:15 catch us the foxes, the little foxes, that ruin the vineyards. NRSV.

480 Here he uses the meeting of the pastor (shepherd) and one church member on the way, the member sings a song "... O Lord your people were missing the path, even the earthly shepherd could not lead them to the right path..... ." After singing that song the pastor respond by singing, "O Lord, I do not know how to preach to the sinners..."

> through others, how can you become real fishers of men? Even the concealed leprosy of Naaman was revealed by the slave girl and the leprosy was healed. God sometimes uses lowly people (p. 6).

Then he summarizes the points by stating, *"To become a real fishers of men, we need to catch our self first; for this God uses other people in our life."* Then he uses another two illustrations, firstly regarding the life history of the one who caught himself first in the El-Bethel camp and became a successful catchers of men. And the other one is the life history of a seller of illicit liquor catching herself in the Camp and becoming a catcher of the rich person whose house she rented.

c. The End

He concludes that catching our self first means to become a fruitful fisher of men. When our weaknesses are revealed, then others will understand and examine themselves and they can realize their weakness and catch themselves. This is true in the life of Simon Peter. He saw himself as unworthy and, 'he fell down at Jesus' knees, saying, and "Go away from me, Lord, for I am a sinful man!"[481] Then Jesus said to Simon, "Do not be afraid; from now on you will be catching people (NRSV)." He catches himself first and he was called to be a fisher of men by Jesus. In the conclusion he identifies himself directly with the campers when he says: *"May the Lord Bless his Word for us all."*[482]

3.4.3. Appraisal of the Sermon

The primary focus of the preacher is to call his listeners to catch themselves first to be able to catch others. It is clearly presented to the audience with the help of illustrations which are actually occurring in the life of some people.

His main focus and purpose is clear. But the illustrations in this sermon were too many. As G. Isaiah stated, some illustrations need to be avoided.[483] There are 12 different illustrations. The length of

481 Luke 5:8, (NRSV).

482 *El-Bethel Magazine* 5/42 (October, 1993): 8.

483 G. Isaiah, *Preach the Word* ..., 120.

the illustrations is not similar: four are long and most of them are short but interesting, impressive, touching, challenging, humorous or refreshing, matching, realistic and supportive to the message. Three of the illustrations are from the Bible; three are from local episodes and the other six are from his personal experiences with his wife. In the six illustrations his wife played prominent role; that could have produce negative attitude from the people since she is the preacher's wife. At the same time the illustrations highlighted that the wife was deeply involved in the personal life of the preacher. As G. Isaiah stated, "Let not your illustrations be too obtrusive."[484] This particular sermon is disturbed by too many illustrations.

The sermon is Topical in type, and it is built around a subject an idea that bears no analytical relation[485] to any one particular passage of scripture and there is no exposition of the text in the sermon. His usual practice of using the text for illustration is found in this sermon. The biblical references are only stated in the conclusion of the sermon which is used for illustration of the one who catches himself first to become the fisher of men.

In the language system, the position of the preacher in this sermon interchanges, some times he used '*we*' (he included himself directly with the audience), '... *our theme*.... (p. 2) ... *we shall*... (p. 2) ... *we took an effort*... (p. 2) ... *we work*... (p. 2) ... *We are not getting*.... (p. 2) ...*we shall try to* (p.2), 'We' is used 27 times in this sermon. Sometimes he uses '*you, your*'... your sin (p. 3) ...*you are blamed* (p. 3) ... *are you a teacher*... (p. 3) ... *your friends*... (p. 3) ... *your secret sins* (p. 3) ... *your inadequacy*... (p. 3) ... *have you ever*.... (p. 3) ...*your fault*... (p. 3) ...*your corruption* (p. 3), *you received*.... (p. 3),... *your friends*....(p. 3), *you will*...(p. 8). This you/your system is mainly used while he challenged the audience; they are not used to show his superiority or inferiority to the audience. 'I' is used more than 16 times; most of them are related to the illustrations of his personal experiences.

484 Ibid., 119.

485 Donald E. Demary, *An Introduction to Homiletics* (Grand Rapids: Baker Book House, 1974), 101.

In this sermon the preacher claimed that he caught himself to catch others, "*At the moment when she catches herself I also catch myself*" (p.5). To the preacher '*catching*' means informing and revealing the negative character and hidden blunder of the person to him/ her, and that should be received positively and made for good use and positive result by the person. This kind of practice may be good for some people but it is not easy to inform and reveal their mistakes to them unless they are mature. As he states, spouse, children and colleagues seem to be helpful for this.

Regarding the organisation, the order of the illustrations is arranged properly. There is no point system in this sermon but this does not mean that it requires it. The purpose of the preacher is well presented; the climax of the sermon is stated in the conclusion of the sermon.

The vocabulary and articulation in the sermon are indigenous, simple, and appropriate with no foreign words to the audience as Perry stated "The language the preacher employs should be contemporary."[486] Sometimes he uses humorous words or sentences appropriately; this does not trouble the flow of the sermon, but is refreshing, and breaks down the defences. John Stott stated, "Laughter has extraordinary power to break down people's defences."[487] The tone of voice was adjusted according to the impression of the statement, and it was audible, but soft, and touching and people could feel that the preacher was really interested in his preaching. People are really controlled by the speech and they were emotionally involved in the preaching mood.

The preacher concluded the sermon by using an illustration and it was exact. As G. Isaiah stated, "the illustration must be exactly on target so that the listeners grasp the meaning in a flash without explanation."[488] And the conclusion leads and convinces the audience to take their obligation in their life.[489] This is related to

486 Lloyd M. Perry and John R. Strubhar, *Evangelistic Preaching* ..., 126.

487 John R. W. Stott, *I Believe in Preaching* (London: Hodder and Stoughton, 1982), 289.

488 G. Isaiah, *Preach the Word* ..., 123.

489 Ralph G. Turnbull, ed., *Baker's Hand Book*..., 61.

Life-Situational preaching. The sermon took 25 minutes, and was suitable to the contemporary world; it is neither too short nor too long.

3.5. Theme: Without the Lad

Biblical Reference: Genesis 44: 30-34, Proverb 22: 6, 24: 11.[490]

3.5.1. Information about the Sermon

The sermon has been taken from *El-Bethel Magazine*, Vol. I, No.3, June1990, 2-8, and the book of *El - Bethel Camp Sermon*, Vol. I, p. 90-100. He preached on 19.1.1990, 6-8 AM in the Camp organized by the Chanmari and Dawrpui Vengthar Pastorate.[491] It was also preached in every El-Bethel Camp, and seems to have been preached more than 220 times in the year 1987-2004.[492]

3.5.2. Formal Elements of Sermon

a. The Beginning

The preacher begins his sermon by reading the Biblical text, and introduces the theme by stating, "Since we claim Christian family is part of our ministry, that is the reason why I included this message concerning Christian family among my messages. The theme of the message will be 'Without the Lad.'

b. The Middle

Then he continued by narrating the story of the texts in the local language. The narration takes half of the sermon:

> ... Now, they took Benjamin to Egypt. In that Judah said, "father, send the boy along with us. If I do not bring him back to you I will bear the blame before you all my life" (Gen. 43:9). What a beautiful speech! Judah made a promise between his father and his beloved son Benjamin; he made himself responsible for any harm that could happen to

490 *El-Bethel Magazine* 1/3 (June 1990): 2-8; K. Lalhmingliana, *El-Bethel Camp Sermon* ..., 90-100.

491 Pi. Chuhveli.

492 K. Hawla Interviewed on 28.4. 2006 at his residence.

> Benjamin saying, "If I do not bring him back to you I will bear the blame before you all my life"... but later they faced troubles.... (p. 91).
>
> They went to Joseph again and prostrated before him. Here we see with prostrating Judah begged Joseph "now therefore, when I come to your servant my father and the lad is not with us, then, as his life is bound up in the lad's life, when he sees that the lad is not with us, he will die; and your servants will bring down the grey hairs of your servant our father with sorrow to Sheol. For your servant became surety for the lad to my father, saying, 'if I do not bring him back to you, then I will bear the blame in the sight of my father all my life. Now therefore, please let your servant remain as a slave to my lord in place of the lad; and let the lad go back with his brothers. For how can I go back to my father if the lad is not with me? I fear to see the suffering that would come upon my father (p. 92-93)."

After narrating the whole story, he points out the faithfulness of Judah in his promise to his father. He remarks, "What a quintessence Judah is! How steadfast he is in his promise to his father!" However, Judah remembered the promise he made to his father, and to fulfil it he begged, "I beseech you my lord, and take me in place of the lad as your slave" (p. 93). Then he applies the passage to the local context of the Christian family:

> Likewise we make promises, when our children are baptized by pastor. Though we accuse pastor as 'irresponsible' when he is not regular in visiting us, but let us consider what we do. We bring our children before the Lord, and we take promise to bring up your child to witness our Lord and saviour Jesus Christ until he grows up?" Do you stand firm in your promise? Do we stand firm in our promise? What exactly is Christian family? I was at families' daily devotion where there were strict observations, made the children fold their hands, and watched them sharply or controlled them with stick...." Have we fulfilled our promise to our

> children? Consider. Even good Christians, spiritual persons and ministers are the ones who often hinder children from coming to Jesus.... On the one hand, we sing happily at the place of fellowship. We cry for the lost souls of those who are in darkness.... (p. 93).

He addresses the local missionary zeal, he did not oppose it but to him family should be the first priority:

> Our hearts fly to faraway lands; perch upon a distant mission field. However, let's say this show how forgetful we are because we never focus our hearts to our family. Let's look around, we do not need to look out from our house, just look in and around our house, we might see scores of our family members who do not know their saviour. Have you ever considered this? Have you stood on your promise too? Your children upon whom you made promise before the Lord are driven towards the land of skull by your enemy, they are dying and many of them have already died. Since you did not work many of them passed away, and some of your children went to the grave because you did not pray for them sincerely.... (p. 94)

He addresses the pattern, type and criteria of Christian family census conducted by the Kohhran Hmeichhia (Church Women Fellowship) to upgrade the Christian life of the society.

> Some are content at having family devotion in the morning and the evening.... But they do not care about how far the devotion touches their family spiritual life. Having a good record family of devotion (in the morning and evening) for Christian family census is not enough.... We feel satisfied at the good outer appearance but are not concerned about the inner decay. (p. 94-95)

He also highlighted the causes of unfruitful ministry of some local preachers and church workers. "We have scores of Christians who do not care about their household, their family members. This is the reason why we cannot show light; did we make God angry because of this? If there's no blessing from your ministry, start making yourself a blessing for your family first, as the passage goes 'tell them what the Lord has done in your life.' We should start from ourselves. And we will bear fruit henceforth" (p. 95-96). He quotes I Timothy 5:8 And whoever does not provide for relatives, and especially for family members, has denied the faith and is worse than an unbeliever (NRSV).

He used an illustration of an English family which is the story of the fasting father who is anxious about the life of his children.[493] And the illustration is applied to the message saying:

> Now, you Christian who have not fasted once for your children, a born again Christian who does not put aside just one night long for your children, even if you decorate the outward appearance of your household, ask yourself whether you have insisted God for the spiritual blessing of your children. Or you would simply blame their friends and say again, "it is because of their companions." We do not know fasting and all night long prayers are sometimes necessary to bring our children to Jesus. Moreover, we do not inculcate good things in their mind other than Sunday school (p. 97).

493 There was a certain Englishman whose children were so wicked. They did not take heed of their father's teaching and advice. At last, he resolved to do something and said, "My dear children, I will neither drink nor eat food till you have new life in your spiritual life." Now he fasted, and he did not eat nor drink for the first day. But he did not stop going to the office for five days.... Now his knees were shaking, and all his strength deserted him. In spite of using cane to help him to walk, his legs were shaking. His children urged him to have food, but he was determined not to eat until there was change in their life and he replied, "I am not having it until there is change in your life. And if I perish, I'll perish for you." They were looking as their father stumbling towards the office. In the meantime, at the porch where they looked at their father, they felt the fellowship of the Holy Spirit and acknowledged their sins. And they called their father, "Father, come back, it is enough, have food now. We acknowledge our sins, what sinners we are!" The man returned home, and they had food together.

He highlights the suffering of the family and challenges the audience to examine their family life carefully by stating:

> Oh! What an abomination our Christian family is! Our grown up children become thorns on our back. Do you know 'you reap what you sowed'? Have you committed your desperation to God? Suppose you stand before God at this moment, you the one who say 'come fast God, we'll be happy,' are you ready for the judgment? Are you really ready at this minute? Will every member of your family be saved? Will some of you be abandoned? Think on it." (p. 98).

Using imagery of the eschaton in relation to the family and stated that:

> Let us imagine God says to us when we parents stand before him, "Welcome, you managed to go through difficulties and distresses on earth and come to heaven. Sit here." He would continue, "Where are your children, the blessings you received from me?" And you answer, "Lord, they are very wicked. All my good advice fell on deaf ears. Besides this, their companions are bad too. So I could not bring them before you." And the Lord would say, "Did I say you can bring them to me? Rather I said you could not do anything without me. Why did you lose them? Didn't I tell you 'let the children come to me, do not hinder them'? And it would be difficult for us to answer Him" (p. 98).

The preacher urged the audience to observe the matter seriously and stated that:

> Do you know a member of your family may depart tonight? You live your life happily without thinking of this. Ironically, you cry when you see Jesus suffer on the cross. Ask him then who is on the cross, he would say, "Daughters of Jerusalem, do not weep for me. Weep for yourselves and for your children." We have scores of ministers, elders, spiritual persons who do not care about the spiritual life of their family. Don't they know the real power of prayer? What

> would be the benefit of the prayer of those who never pray all night long for their family, and who do not care about their family? (p. 99)

c. The End

The preacher concludes the sermon by stating how to pray to the Lord, "Lord, I do not have any concern for the children you have blessed me with my heart. I cannot bring them before you. Give me a heart to understand their preciousness to you." He assures their prayer would be answered by stating, "Your prayer will be answered." He repeated the same question; "would your family be saved if God comes at this hour? Are you really ready? As for me and my family I assure you we will be saved if you ask me the same question." (p.100) He invited the audience to take this matter seriously in their future ministry. "With contemplating this, let us proceed towards heaven. May the Lord bless His holy word for us all. AMEN."

3.5.3. Appraisal of the Sermon

The main focus of the sermon is to keep the promise, vowed in the church, by looking after the children according to the will of God. For this he uses a Biblical illustration of the vow made by Judah to his father and his faithfulness to the promise. The presentation was orderly arranged and it was fascinatingly narrated by the preacher. The vocabulary is impressive and the expression striking to the audience.

The preacher quotes words from three hymns:

> **1**. "Look out and see those who do not know their saviour.
> They remain there calmly without knowing the saviour.
> There's no one to lead them: they do not know the saviour,
> Go fast and preach the gospel."[494] (p. 94)

494 Composed by Laibata, No 390, *Presbyterian Kohhran leh Mizoram Baptist Kohhran Kristian Hla Bu* (Aizawl: Synod Literature and Publication Board, 2004), 422.

2. 'Come fast God, we'll be happy'[495] (p. 98)
3. Each family is lessening,
When a member departs,
Will there be a time that all the beloved members of the family
Are there in the eternal heaven?[496] (p. 100)

The hymns quoted are supportive, relevant and helpful to touch the sentiments of the audience. This type of preaching is popular among the Mizo evangelists.

Unlike other sermons, the preacher used only two illustrations but they were long; one is from the text itself and another one is the story about the English father who fasted for repentance of his children. Indigenous illustration was not used, as well as his personal experiences were not much shared in this sermon. Both of the illustrations were relevant. At the same time in the second illustration we do not find the repentance of the children. It was stated up to the acknowledgement that they are sinners. If it was presented fully including their repentance it would have been more convincing and would have been an excellent illustration.

The application part is strong, direct to the point and fearless as John R. Strubhar says, "Evangelistic style should be direct and fearless,"[497] relevant and matching to the context. Since, there are many parents neglecting caring for their children, resulting in drug addiction, alcoholism, stealing, loose living and failure in education, as well as increasing of Commercial Sex Workers in the society.

The preacher's perspective on the society seems to be negative, as well towards the efforts made by the Church Women Fellowship towards the empowerment of the Christian family. That can denigrate the service rendered by the women. So, in this regard he needs to be more thoughtful of it.

495 Composed by Rev. J Cennick, Translated by Rev. Liangkhaia, No. 240, *Presbyterian Kohhran leh Mizoram Baptist Kohhran Kristian Hla Bu* (Aizawl: Synod Literature and Publication Board, 2004), 259.

496 Composed by Ada R. Habershon translated by Thanga, No. 489, *Presbyterian Kohhran leh Mizoram Baptist Kohhran Kristian Hla Bu* (Aizawl: Synod Literature and Publication Board, 2004), 529.

497 Lloyd M. Perry and John R. Strubhar, *Evangelistic Preaching* ..., 129.

In this sermon the preacher confined himself with the audience stating 'us, we, *our,' our…* (p. 90), *we used to include…* (p. 90), *if we see….* (p. 91), *we took a vow…* (p. 93), *we blame….* (p. 93), *our Christian family…* (p. 93), *we control…* (p. 93), *our promise….* (p. 94). At the same time he urged the audience by using 'You,' and asking challenging questions…. *Do you stand firm in your promise? …. Do we stand firm in our promise? … What exactly is Christian family?* (p. 93). *Do you fulfil your promise in your household?* (p. 95) *Are you honest in your promise? And do you justify yourself?* (p. 96) *Are you really ready at this minute? Will every member of your family be saved? Will some of you be abandoned?* (p. 98) *Would your family be saved if God comes at this hour? Are you really ready?* (p. 100) These questions are not to be responded to on the spot, but to help the audience for self evaluation of their past acts in relation to their care of their children. It might be helpful but it may have disturbed the exposition of the text. But it seems that to the preacher that it worked for his purpose.

Through the video recording, it can be stated that the voice was not very clear due to continuous preaching, but it was audible.[498] His posture was relevant to the word and expression. He was very serious in his preaching; because of this, drew the attention of the people. All the gestures of the preacher were from within him and are varied but helpful for communicating the meaning of the message.[499] Since he masters the sermons, eye contact was regular and covered the entire audience. It is natural, straight and personal.[500] The dress and appearance was moderate.

The preacher concludes the sermon by using the type *making an application,*[501] and invitation. To Lloyd M. Perry and John R. Strubhar, inviting the audience in the conclusion of the sermon is 'an appropriate and biblical, essential, historically proved method of

498 W.E Sangster, *The Craft of the Sermon* (London: The Epworth Press, 1964), 187.

499 Viggo Sogaard, *Media in Church and Mission: Communicating the Gospel* (California: William Carey Library, 1993), 37.

500 G. Isaiah, *Preach the Word…*, 130.

501 Ibid., 123.

bringing men to Christ.'[502] The sermon took 26 minutes, and it was suitable to the contemporary audience.

II. Conclusion

The preaching ministry of K. Lalhmingliana is directly related to the camp ministry. Camp contains counselling class with a particular theme which is significant for self evaluation for the campers. All K. Hminga's seventy sermons are related to the practical and social issues. The spiritual dynamic in the preaching is beyond our purview and separate, since the involvement of the Holy Spirit is immeasurable, and is beyond the system.[503]

Regarding the *theme* and *selection of texts* of the sermons, since he was a revival preacher, most of the preaching was to revive the spiritual life of the people thus making them care, worry and love of the sinners with a new heart. The 'Theme' of the sermons and preaching directly related to social issues and spiritual life of the people. Corresponding to the theme, he chose the Biblical Texts. Thus the themes determine the Biblical Text. He was a craftsman in preparation like W. E. Sangster.[504] The theme based on the Biblical text is then expounded with the help of various illustrations. Because of the domination of the theme and motto of the Team, K. Hminga mainly chose only a single verse or a few verses from the Bible as his Biblical text. Like the independent preacher Sadhu Sunder Singh,[505] K. Hminga seems to give more importance to the theme and the nature of his audience than the Biblical text of his sermon.

An examination of the sermons of K. Lalhmingliana has revealed that he uses simple but relevant vocabulary. Sometimes he used the conversational form of speech by putting questions to his hearers and addressing them directly as "you." K. Hminga never apologized

502 Lloyd M. Perry & John R. Strubhar, *Evangelistic Preaching* ..., 107-109.

503 Jay E. Adams, *Sermon Analysis* (Denver: Accent Publications, Inc., 1986), 16.

504 Horton Davies, *Varieties of English Preaching 1900-1969* (London: SCM Press, 1963), 209.

505 Perumalla Surya Prakash, *The Preaching of Sadhu Sunder Singh,* (Bangalore: Wordmakers, 1991), 155.

in his sermon.[506] He never imitated other preachers.[507] He was good in application. Using relevant illustrations from his life experiences was one of his strengths in his preaching. At the same time glorifying oneself in preaching is not appreciated by W. E. Sangster, saying "Don't glorify yourself,"[508] since it could lead to self advertisement not Christ.

One of his weak points is Biblical exegesis and systematic exposition. As stated 'Exegesis is usually neglected,'[509] K. Hminga uses Bible but not for exposition but still uses for a starting point in his preaching as P. T. Forsyth says 'Bible is still the preacher's starting-point.'[510] The preacher did not give much importance to the exposition of the texts but give more importance to the theme and the message. This type of preaching does not enrich the audience in the biblical knowledge, but it confined to the message of the sermon.

The sermons are not boring; rather they are interesting, challenging, and relevant to the contemporary situation of the audience. Some of the illustrations in single sermons are too many, that can disturb the message of the sermon, but obvious since they are the personal experiences of the preacher. K. Hminga was against the suggestion of W. E. Sangster regarding repetition of sermon,[511] but he was glowing to it, and repeated many times as was already highlighted in the information about the sermons.

Delivery of the sermons is convincing and similar to all his sermons. The preacher is confident in his preaching since he preached the same sermon many times. He was well versed on the content. This helps the preacher to make his voice attractive and charming.

The preacher always confines himself with the people; that pull the people towards his side when he used 'we', 'us', and 'our.' This pattern elevates the people towards deeper self examination that

---

506 W. E. Sangster, *The Craft…*, 184.

507 Ibid., 195.

508 Ibid., 291.

509 Rev. H. Zalawma Rev. H & Rev. H. Vanlalruata, *An Introduction to Worship and Preaching* (Aizawl: Aizawl Theological College, 2005), 145.

510 P. T. Forsyth, *Positive Preaching and the Modern Mind* (Michigan: Baker Book House, 1980), 8.

511 W. E Sangster, *The Craft…*, 194.

cause positive result, awareness, and repentance. Sometimes he used the conversational form of speech by putting questions to his hearers and addressing them directly as "you."

The sermons are mainly related to the excessive involvement of the human being rather than the work of the Holy Spirit. But this does not mean that he was denying the role of the Holy Spirit. To him, the durable effort of the human being is blessed by the Holy Spirit. Because of this he uses 'you,' many times in his sermons to motivate the audience. This is the indigenous evangelical type of sermon.

His voice was audible, facial expression and gestures relevant, and convincing. His gestures are from within himself, and varied. The eye contact was natural, straight and personal to the audience.

He did not employ the methods of analogy and of interpretation. He always had a short formal introduction to his sermons. The basic frame work of his preaching consisted of personal statements, illustrations, and interpretation with application to his hearers.

The next chapter will deal the homiletic structure and illustrations in the sermons.

Chapter 4

The Homiletic Structure and the Illustrations

I. Introduction

This chapter consist the homiletic structure of the indigenous sermons by K. Hminga and also deals with the application of illustrations in the sermons along with type and sources. It is followed by summary of chapter.

1. The Homiletic Structure

The form of the introduction, the conclusion and the development (explanation) of the sermon by K. Hminga is discussed below.

1.1. The Introduction

Normally 'the content of the introduction should clarify the purpose of the message,'[512] but K. Lalhmingliana is not used to having long and formal introductions to his sermons, but 'brief.'[513] Most of the time he began by reading the Biblical text, and he introduced the theme, "we shall just name the theme...." then he directs to the main

512 Lloyd John Ogilvie, "Introducing the Sermon," *Hand Book of Contemporary Preaching*, edited by Michael Duduit (Wheaton: Broadman Press, 1992), 177.

513 Donald E. Demary, *An Introduction to Homiletics...*, 76.

body. It may be due to the limitation of time or because he did not feel it necessary, since he often preaches on the same topic in various Gospel Campaigns and Camps.

1.2. The Conclusion

The conclusion was not mentioned earlier. As G. Isaiah suggested, he never mentions "finally," or "in conclusion,"[514] he just suddenly summarizes the sermon within one sentence without informing the audience and says, "*May the Lord bless His holy word for us all,* AMEN." This rapid closing of the sermon always surprises the audience. Two elements are noticeable in most of the conclusions of the sermons of K. Lalhmingliana.

1.2.1. Through Exhortation: After summarization of the content he usually invites the audience to take a fresh step for the future ministry; this is found in 'Without the Lad',[515] 'Window to the World,'[516] 'The Christian Life: Two Ways to Ruin,'[517] 'Enemy of the Cross,'[518] 'The painful heart of the loser.'[519] As L. Harbour says, "the conclusion needs to be understandable.... The congregation needs to clearly understand what you are challenging them to do,"[520] most of the conclusion of K. Hminga's sermons are clear and easy to understand.

1.2.2. Summarization: Sometimes he concludes the sermon by using 'it will happen in such manner.' This can be called general statement of the conclusion, this is an affirmation of the sermon, which is found in 'Cross, the Powerlessness of God,'[521] 'The Life that Negates

514 G. Isaiah, *Preach the Word...*, 124.

515 *El-Bethel Magazine* 1/3 (June, 1990): 8; K. Lalhmingliana, *El-Bethel Camp Sermon ...*, 100.

516 K. Lalhmingliana, *El-Bethel Camp Sermon ...*, 110.

517 *El-Bethel Magazine* 2/13 (May, 1991): 6; K. Lalhmingliana, *El-Bethel Camp Sermon ...*, 139.

518 *El-Bethel Magazine* 2/7 (October, 1990): 6; K. Lalhmingliana, *El-Bethel Camp Sermon ...*, 147.

519 *El-Bethel Magazine* 3/21, (January, 1992), 6.

520 Brian L. Harbour, "Concluding the Sermon," *Hand Book of Contemporary Preaching*, edited by Michael Duduit (Wheaton: Broadman Press, 1992), 227.

521 *El-Bethel Magazine* 2/15 (July, 1991):7; K. Lalhmingliana, *El-Bethel Camp Sermon ...*, 156.

Comforts,'[522] 'The Captive life,'[523] 'The Path of the Children of the Cross,'[524] 'The Great Banquet of God,'[525] 'Holy Spirit the giver of Life.'[526] As already stated, he always included himself with the audience, by stating "*May the Lord bless His holy word for us all,*" AMEN."

1.3. The Explanation of the Theme

Most of the sermons are topical by structure. The themes of the sermons are given more importance than the texts of the sermon. Expository type of preaching was not practiced by him. All the Biblical references for the sermon are used for illustrations of the message. Generally he chose a text and draws a theme or topic out of it. The sermons do not contain sub topic nor sub headlines. Most of the content of the sermons is under one theme, and that was the main theme of the sermon.

There was no system or consistency in the structure. But there was a form and unity in his sermon in which the entire sermons are under the main theme without having sub topic or sub point. This is the peculiarity of his sermons. From the beginning of the introduction, the sermon focuses on one particular goal. To reach such destination, relevant illustrations are collected and applied to it. But there is no methodical application and in some sermons there are many illustrations, e.g. in 'Fishers of Men,' twelve illustrations are used, but in some sermons few illustrations are used e.g. 'Without the lad,' there are only two illustrations.

---

522 *El-Bethel Magazine* 1/6 (September, 1990), 7; K. Lalhmingliana, *El-Bethel Camp Sermon ...*, 130.

523 *El-Bethel Magazine* 2/19 (November, 1991), 5; K. Lalhmingliana, *El-Bethel Camp Sermon ...* 119.

524 *El-Bethel Magazine*2/12 (March & April, 1991), 9; K. Lalhmingliana, *El-Bethel Camp Sermon ...* 167.

525 *El-Bethel Magazine* 2/16 (August, 1991), 10; K. Lalhmingliana, *El-Bethel Camp Sermon ...*, 197.

526 *El-Bethel Magazine* 7/17 (September, 1991), 7; K. Lalhmingliana, *El-Bethel Camp Sermon ...*, 43.

2. The Illustrations

The language of illustrations plays a dominant role in the preaching of K. Lalhmingliana. He uses illustrations from the Bible, his personal experiences and his observation of nature as well as experiences from other people. His examples and illustrations make his sermon interesting, attractive, illuminating the message, and making the message easy to memorise and to make plain the obscure, as G. Isaiah says, "illustration throws light on the concepts of the message,"[527] his illustrations illuminate the message. Three types of illustrations can be found in the sermons of K. Lalhmingliana – Biblical, personal experiences and those that are drawn from other sources.

2.1. Biblical Illustrations: As Baumann says, "Bible is the prime source,"[528] K. Hminga also uses quotations and stories from the Bible to support his speech. For, Example *"He has gone to be the guest of one who is a sinner,"*[529] "*For the Son of Man came to seek out and to save the lost.*"[530] "*Vengeance is mine, I will repay.*"[531] '*You hypocrite, first take the log out of your own eye, and then you will see clearly to take the speck out of your neighbor's eye.*'[532] As it is already included in chapter three most of the illustrations used by him is from the Bible, and are biographical[533] and some are parables of Jesus Christ, for example, The Lost Coin, the Lost Sheep, The story of the encounter of Zachaeus and Jesus, Dry Bones in the valley, [534] Lot's wife,[535] The

527 G. Isaiah, *Preach the Word*..., 113.

528 J. Daniel Baumann, *An Introduction to Contemporary Preaching* (Grand Rapids: Baker Book House, 1981), 175.

529 *NRSV*. Humility: 'The Gospel that reaches Sinners' Luke 19:7.

530 *NRSV* on the sermon 'Humility-The Gospel that Reaches Sinners' K. Lalhmingliana, *El-Bethel Camp Sermon*, Vol. I ..., 7. Luke 19:10.

531 Hebrew 10:29. K. Lalhmingliana, *El-Bethel Camp Sermon* ..., 109.

532 Matthew 7:5, K. Lalhmingliana, *El-Bethel Camp Sermon*..., 116.

533 G. Isaiah, *Preach the Word*..., 117.

534 Lalhmingliana, *El-Bethel Camp Sermon*..., 212.

535 Ibid., 132.

life of Nicodemus,[536] The life of Peter,[537] The life history of Jacob,[538] The life of king David.[539]

The use of scriptural illustrations in preaching is considered a good notion because "Biblical illustrations will increase overall Biblical literacy, or an idea that scripture alone can rightly interpret scripture."[540] But there is a problem in quoting from the Bible too. Surya Prakash says, "If the congregation is not well-acquainted with the Bible, they will have difficulty in following the preacher."[541] But fortunately, most of the audience in the camp are familiar with Biblical verses, since most of them are Christians.

2.2. Personal Experience: K. Hminga uses personal material drawn from his own life experience as he was truly aman of indigenous thought by nature. His personal illustrations begin as follows: 'Before I receive the anointing of the Holy Spirit…,' '*One day the Holy Spirit devastated my life…*,'[542] '*When I erected my Father's tomb stone…*'[543], '*When I visited the camp with commercial sex workers…*,'[544] '*I use to torture the drug addicts, alcoholics…*;'[545] '*When I was in Thingsulthliah in 1981…*,'[546] '*When I was in Burma…*,'[547] '*One day I rode a bicycle….*,'[548] '*One day a wretched father came to me…*'[549] '*My wife is also intelligent to some extent….*'[550]

536 Ibid., 209.

537 Ibid., 211.

538 Ibid., 238.

539 Ibid., 14.

540 D. Buttric, *Homiletic: Moves and Structure* (Philadelphia: Fortress Press, 1987), 145.

541 Perumalla Surya Prakash, *The Preaching of Sadhu Sunder Singh* (Bangalore: Wordmakers, 1991), 270.

542 K. Lalhmingliana, *El-Bethel Camp Sermon* …, 2.

543 Ibid., 216.

544 Ibid., 230.

545 Ibid., 1.

546 Ibid., 25.

547 Ibid., 36.

548 Ibid., 35.

549 Ibid., 60.

550 Ibid., 66.

Using personal experiences in the preaching might be contrasting to the opinion of John the Baptist, in referring to Christ; 'He must increase, but I must decrease.'[551] W. E. Sangster says, "talking overmuch about oneself is a fearful fault in a preacher.'[552] Buttric also says, 'Though illustrations come to mind and may often be drawn from our own experience, we do not have to talk about ourselves in sermons no matter how exhilarating it may be. Personal illustrations always split focus.'[553] But this opinion appears to be too rigid;[554] using personal experience of a preacher in illustrations is convincing, meaningful, practical, and is always considered a strong point in Christian preaching.

2.3. Other Sources: The following illustrations are introduced from other sources, like books, stories, incidents, by K. Hminga, e. g. The lady who support the drug addicts;[555] Persecution of Christians in Rumania;[556] Rev. Paul in America;[557] The Uniform of Army Officer;[558] The visit to China by two friends;[559] the Poor Widow;[560] The Old Women in Scandinavia,[561] The anxious English father.[562] Mostly the preacher uses illustrations from the Bible, since "the Bible is the source of preaching and the sustainer of preachers"[563] and his personal experiences, only few illustrations are used from other sources.

---

551 John3:30, *The New Revised Standard Version*, (Nashville, TN: Thomas Nelson Publishers), 1989.

552 W.E Sangster, *The Craft*..., 226.

553 D. Buttric, *Homiletic* ..., 143.

554 Perumalla Surya Prakash, *The Preaching of Sadhu Sunder Singh* ..., 272.

555 K. Lalhmingliana, *El-Bethel Camp Sermon* ..., 71.

556 Ibid., 127.

557 Ibid., 171.

558 Ibid., 173-174.

559 Ibid., 24.

560 Ibid., 84.

561 Lalhmingliana, *"Tuihna Kang Ngailo Nun (The Life of a Never Ending Fountain)" El-Bethel Magazine* 1/4 (July 1990): 3-13; K. Lalhmingliana, *El-Bethel Camp Sermon* ..., 62-79.

562 Lalhmingliana, *El- Bethel Camp Sermon* ..., 96.

563 Richard Lischer, *A Theology of Preaching* (Nashville: Abingdon, 1981), 95.

II. Summary

K. Hminga never uses long introduction in his preaching. In the conclusion he mainly follows two types of conclusion one is exhortation and another one is summarization. His conclusion of the sermon is short but appealing and convincing.

The study reveals that K. Hminga uses simple home-grown but relevant vocabularies and the 'radiant words'[564] that tend to stimulate faith, hope and courage. Sometime he uses the conversational form of speech by putting questions to his hearers and addressing them directly as "you." He does not employ the methods of analogy and of interpretation.

From the above discussion we can summarize that, K. Hminga uses a variety of illustrations in his preaching to make the sermon interesting to illuminate the messages to the audience with indigenous roots. The study commission report also comments on his usage of illustrations and stated that, "All the illustrations were really illuminating to the sermon and it enhances clarity of the message."[565] The basic framework of his preaching consists of introduction, body, conclusion, personal statements, illustrations and interpretation with application to his hearers. The next chapter deals with the theology of the El-Bethel team.

---

564 James W. Cox, "Evaluating the Sermon," *Hand Book of Contemporary Preaching*, edited by Michael Duduit (Wheaton: Broadman Press, 1992), 233

565 The Report of the Study Commission (Aizawl Theological College Faculty), on the Bethel Revival Movement, p. 4 (unpublished).

Chapter 5

Theology of El-Bethel Evangelistic Team

I. Introduction

This portion is an attempt to study the characteristics of the unique Bethel Revival theology from Christian theological perspective. This revival movement has expressed and affected the Mizo spirituality. So, it is an attempt to highlight the particular teaching of El-Bethel Team and try to compare with Christian theological doctrines.

1. The Seeds of Faith

The Seeds of Faith (SoF) system was started by this El-Bethel Team in Mizoram. There is a uniqueness of Bethel Revival from the earlier revivals,[566] which was 'a most striking character of Bethel Revival Movement.'[567] Individual prayer was highly involved in the SoF method and it is based on some Biblical verses.[568]

566 First Revival (1906), Second Revival (1913), Third Revival (1919-1923), Fourth Revival (1935), Fifth Revival (1984) Rev. Lalnghinglova, *Zoram Nghahchhan* (Aizawl: Saikungi, 1993), 138.

567 R. Vanlaltluanga, "Revival Movements"..., 31. (Unpublished).

568 Some give freely, yet grow all the richer; others withhold what is due, and only suffer want. A generous person will be enriched and one who gives water will get water" (Proverb 11:24-26). "Honor the LORD with your substance and with the first fruits of all your produce; then your barns will be filled with

As Richard Lischer states, "People listen to preaching only when they are convinced that it is the word of God."[569] Listening to the teaching, campers were much convinced by it. Campers dropped their precious belongings in the designated container,[570] expecting the immediate blessings of God, since they were taught that the more they give their valuables and belongings by faith they will soon and surely get the return blessing from God.[571] Some mentioned specific reasons in their prayers before they dropped their offerings in the SoF container.[572] Campers dropped their belongings such as money, jacket, shawls, blankets, jewelleries, clothes, sweaters, coats, watches, shoes.[573] Some wrote names of what they wanted to give and later they were collected by the responsible persons, e.g., cow, vehicles, pig,[574] etc. Some accept that SoF practice works and is effective.[575]

---

plenty, and your vats will be bursting with wine" (Proverb 3:9-10). "Give and it will be given to you. A good measure, pressed down, shaken together, running over, will be put into your lap; for the measure you give will be the measure you get back." (Luke 6:39). "Bring the full tithe into the storehouse, so that there may be food in my house, and thus put me to the test, says the LORD of hosts; see if I will not open the windows of heaven for you and pour down for you an overflowing blessing (Malachi 3:10). Rinna Thlai Chi (The Seeds of Faith)." *El-Bethel Magazine* 2/20 (December 1991), 11.

569 Richard Lischer, *A Theology of Preaching ...*, 66.

570 *Forum* No.8 (April 1990): 2; *Forum* No.12 (April, 1990), 5.

571 "Rinna Thlai Chi (The Seed Faith)" *El-Bethel Magazine* 2/ 20, (December, 1991), 11.

572 J. Malsawma stated that, "I mentioned five reasons of dropping my money in the Seeds of Faith, and then I went for Bethel Prayer." J. Malsawma, "Testimony (El-Bethel Camp at Tanhril)," *El-Bethel Magazine* 2/13, April and (May, 1991), 6-11. The father of C. Lalramthangi of Thimphu (Bhutan) gives three reasons: first, for his conversion, second, so there will be no problems in his salary and thirdly to give him daughter, he mentioned that all the three reasons were answered and everything was alright. The father of C Lalramthangi, "the Letter to the Speaker," *El-Bethel Magazine* 2/19, (November, 1991), 11.

573 "West Phaileng El-Bethel Camp," *El-Bethel Magazine* 2/11, (February, 1991), 16.

574 "Thingsai Pastor Bial El-Bethel Camp Report," *El-Bethel Magazine* 2/11, (February, 1991), 15.

575 Upa V. Neihkunga, interview on 28.4.2006. "Rinna Thlai Chi (The Seeds of Faith)" *El-Bethel Magazine* 2/20, (December, 1991), 11. Rothangliani of New

When they were answered in their purpose some were proud that their will was fulfilled.[576]

Offerings were not by compulsion but by being aware of the teaching of the SoF. Money received by the SoF was utilized for the expenses incurred in the camp and helping the El-Bethel Team, helping NGOs and some other agencies.

SoF has a historical background in the teachings of Oral Robert.[577] Lalchungnunga and K. Lalhmingliana started using it in 1984 at Tahan, Burma.[578] K. Hminga himself practices this SoF in his personal life, based on Proverbs 11: 24-25.[579] The book *Miracle of Seed Faith* by Oral Robert was translated by Rev. Zokima in 1986.[580] Since then this teaching was widely spread. In 1990 the same book *Miracle of Seed Faith* was translated by Malsawmdawngliana in Mizo, Published by K. Lalhmachhuani of Aizawl. It was reprinted and 2nd edition was released on Dec. 2000. Authorization statement from the author or publisher in this translated book is not found.

This is new *Doctrine of Giving* being taught to the people. "We need to give an offering, expecting the return from God."[581] The whole idea was summed up by Vanlaltluanga; to him, "offerings should be made with the expectation of returned blessings, mostly materialistic."[582] This SoF teaching can be studied by the following.

This SoF teaching was new for the local people, Vanlallawma says, "This new method of giving to the Lord, teaches the people *a new name for giving*, *new motive of giving* and *new end of giving*."[583]

Khawlek gave her clothes in the Seeds of Faith for the recovery of her son and her son was found recovered. Rothangliani, "Testimony," *El-Bethel Magazine* 5/56, (December, 1994), 16-17.

576 C. Lalthuama "El-Bethel atanga Kan mize lan theihna te," (The appearance of our character through El-Bethel), point no. 43:5 (Unpublished).

577 C. Vanlallawma, *Bethel Revival*..., 10.

578 C. Vanlallawma, *Bethel Revival* ..., 13, V. L. Zaikima, *Ka Tla Fai Ta*..., 89.

579 V. L. Zaikima, *Ka Tla Fai Ta*... 89.

580 C. Vanlallawma, *Bethel Revival* ..., 13.

581 Ibid., 9.

582 R. Vanlaltluanga, "Revival Movements"..., 31.

583 C. Vanlallawma, *Bethel Revival* ..., 14.

A New Name for Giving: The name itself, 'Seeds of Faith,' to cover all types of giving to God, demands the return blessing of God out of the gift. Returns were expected not for others but for the giver[584] and the gifts are expected in material things and not spiritual. But the name itself does not have a place for the one who gives the offering out of love, donation, and charity.

A New Motive of Giving: The SoF is related to a new motive of giving. Here the motive of giving is to multiply the gift by God. Humans do not have the authority to insist that God multiplies whatever is given to Him.

A New End of Giving: This is related to the result of giving, for the one who gives the offering**.** The ideology of this method can be compared with buying a lottery ticket; it is not for the glory of God but for the material benefits of the giver. Here the theology is Self-Centred Living.[585] God is not glorified and it is not safe for the Christians. Vanlallawma stated that, "This kind of teaching is new to the people, so it is noteworthy to the churches and difficult to understand for the churches."[586] *The Bethesda* (Weekly News), of 7th October 1989 with the headline "*Let us be Careful*" mentioned that: "... nowadays many church members... do not think about offering, whether it is Biblical or not....." At the same time K. Lianthanga was also against this type of preaching and called it as *Simonism* based on Acts 8:18-20;[587] he stated that, "this is heresy from the time of apostles trying to buy the power of God by money."[588]

In the song composed by Lalthuama, titled 'the Seeds of Faith,' C. Lalthuama named the Seeds of Faith as "*the trap of Diabol*,"[589]

584 Ibid.

585 Ibid.

586 C. Vanlallawma, *Bethel Revival* ...., 10.

587 Now when Simon saw that the Spirit was given through the laying on of the apostles' hands, he offered them money, saying, "Give me also this power so that anyone on whom I lay my hands may receive the Holy Spirit."[20] But, Peter said to him, "May your silver perish with you, because you thought you could obtain God's gift with money (NRSV).

588 Cited from K. Lianthanga "Rinna Thlai Chi Tuh" *Bethesda* (14 October, 1989), by V. L Zaikima, *Ka Tla Fai Ta*... 148.

589 C. Lalthuama, *El-Bethel Camp Hla*..., 6th Stanza.

"*The enemy of the Cross,*" "*the resources of Satan feast,*"[590] "*the magic box of Burma* (Myanmar)."[591] This perspective shows that it has some negative result.

There can be some similarity with the *indulgence* in Church History which was one of the main reasons of Reformation, in relation to the purpose of giving. This is denied by the El-Bethel Publication Board, which states that:

> All the blessings, the power of God, salvation of human beings, healing, physical blessings, intelligence, etc, cannot be bought by earthly money…; this Seeds of Faith is not related to selling and buying a thing. The theology of Seeds of Faith is an extreme definition of the offering to God. It teaches us that when we make an offering of something big to God, it gives us more inner satisfaction than when we give something small.[592]

From the above statement, it can be noticed that wherever more money or other valuable belongings are spent, it draws more attention to it. C. Lalthuama stated that '*Whoever drops big amounts of offering will receive the blessings of God immediately, but those who offer less than they can will not receive the same immediately.*'[593] If a person gives more he is supposed to get more; it may be true, but if such is the case there will be no chances for the poor, as they do not have big amount to give God. Then their prayers will not be effective since they give less than the rich people. Then God will not be the God of the poor, so there will be discrimination in answering the prayer of the people. Such is not acceptable, since God loves all people equally and died for all. The action of God cannot be measured on the basis of the amount of gift given by human beings. We human beings are unworthy, but only by His love and grace we are reconciled to him.

---

590 Ibid., 7th Stanza.

591 Ibid., 9th Stanza.

592 "Rinna Thlai Chi (The Seed Faith) *El-Bethel Magazine* 2/20 (December, 1991), 11-12.

593 C. Lalthuama, *El- Bethel Camp Hla* (*The song of El-Bethel Camp*) 13th Stanza (unpublished).

The money spent in the SoF relates the faith of the person to the Holy Spirit. Vanlaltluanga stated that, "They connected the idea with the coming of the Holy Spirit."[594] At Tanhril camp held in Nov.1989, it was said 'that the Holy Spirit did not come because the SoF was very little,[595] and they collected it again.'[596] This shows that they believed the involvement of the Holy Spirit was directly related to the contribution of the campers through the SoF; if this is so then the campers are controlling the activity of the Holy Spirit, which is not easy to accept.

It is impossible to know exactly whether God answers according to the amount they give through the SoF. in the camp most of the campers gave through the SoF, but some returned empty handed, without receiving the new inspiration of the Holy Spirit. They could not offer *thanksgiving prayer,*[597] which can cause further spiritual backsliding as well as suspicion about the power of God.[598] The study commission report also states that "there can be a danger in the teaching of SoF that can misguide our faith towards God in relation to giving offering." [599]

The Christian offering to God is related with submission to God. Giving is the nature of God that is attached in the nature of men by God; humans are called to give our hearts to him, to help and support others, to share and pray for others. Giving offering is an act of worship, it is a thanksgiving offering, and it is for the glory of God. Giving also indicates the loyalty of the believers to

---

594 R. Vanlaltluanga, Revival Movement"..., 31; Personal interview with C. Lalthuama on 28.5.2006.

595 C. Lalthuama, *El-Bethel Camp Hla...,* 13th Stanza. (unpublished).

596 Personal interview with C. Lalthuama on 28.5.2006.

597 After the Bethel Prayer is over all the campers returned to the place called RV. There they are asked by the Prayer Machine whether they are successful in their prayer (Bethel) or not. If the camper say 'yes' then he/ she was asked to pray Thanksgiving Prayer, but many campers answers are negative and they could not offer Thanksgiving Prayer. This occurrence shows the camper was not successful in the camp and need to come again in the next camp.

598 V. L. Zaikima, *Ka Tla Fai Ta...* 153.

599 The Report of the Study Commission (Aizawl Theological College Faculty), on the Bethel Revival Movement, 1990:5. (unpublished).

God. The Christian giving does not much emphasise the return from God, but is given because of love and for the extension of the Kingdom of God, not expecting the return blessing to the giver, but sometimes for others. But in the SoF all the returns will be received by the giver him/herself. It places the giver in the centre, not the one to whom we give or the others. It has taught self-centred living, which is opposed to the doctrine of incarnation, the *kenosis* of Jesus Christ, the foundation of our faith. Therefore, it is not acceptable and cannot be justified as it is. On the other hand, this teaching awakes the people in the knowledge of giving offerings and Church offerings were increased'[600] through this ministry. But this positive result does not mean that SoF teaching is safe for the church. It certainly indicates people were revived in their spiritual lives.

2. The Bethel Prayer

Bethel prayer is one of the new contributions of El-Bethel Team among the Mizo Christians. It is one of the most dominating features of the Bethel revival. Many campers benefited from Bethel Prayer.[601] The word 'Bethel' for the team meant 'serious individual prayer' in remote places or forests, as stated in chapter two. The Team divided all the campers into many different groups under the leadership from the Team members, each group had around 40 members or so.[602] Before they went to their selected places, each group was informed a particular place called R.V. in which all the group members were to return after their prayers. Then all campers were sent out within the appointed area to pray independently and seriously.

600 The fruit of the Bethel Revival Movement in the church's offerings is like this: The 1990-1991 Synod Budget was Rs. 4, 98, 73, 000. 00 The actual income was Rs. 5, 47, 36, 741. 78; the budget was crossed by Rs. 48, 63, 741. 78." Bethel Thunawi," *El-Bethel Magazine* 2/14 (June, 1991), 14.

601 R. Vanlaltluanga, "Revival Movements"..., 33.

602 K. Hawla Sailo, "El- Bethel Harhna"..., 548.

2.1. Prayer Slogans

The leader[603] taught them a prayer slogan[604] and compelled them to raise their arms upwards, to follow his words accordingly with a loud voice before each departed for his independent prayer. The content of the prayer slogans were different according to the spiritual status of the camper, divided into four categories:[605]

2.1.1. Ministers: Here 'ministers' mean all church workers assigned in different responsibilities in the local church's ministry.[606] The main focus of the prayer slogan[607] is to help the campers to discover and confess their weak and ineffective ministry.

2.1.2. Alcoholics, Drug Addicts, CSW, Illicit Liquor Sellers and Makers: Their prayer slogan was formulated by the group leaders by considering their spiritual condition. The main focus of the prayer slogan[608] is to pray to God to rescue them from the bondage of their slavery.

---

603 Leaders are from the Team members 'Tawngtai Khawl' (Prayer Machine), newly reborn young persons from the El-Bethel Camp who do not have much experience in Christian life. They were previously drug addicts, alcoholics, and few of them are mature in Christian life. Rev. C. Vanlalhruaia interviewed on 13.6.2006.

604 K. Hawla Sailo, "El- Bethel Harhna"..., 548.

605 V. L. Zaikima, *Ka Tla Fai Ta...* 98.

606 Some of their responsibilities are e.g., Sunday School Teachers, Preachers, Bible Readers, and Wednesday Night Theme Opener, and all other responsible persons in various ministries.

607 O Lord! I, your unworthy servant used to be proud of being called your servant. I served you only by name in the sight of others, but my inner life is more dangerous than the disease of cancer and I served you for my good reputation and not for Christ's sake; I served you with my external good human nature but without inner righteousness, 'I have served you without receiving the Baptism of the Holy Spirit, and all my previous ministries are a waste of time and useless.' I was appointed by the favour of the church committee not by the recognition of the Holy Spirit. O Lord, I request you to make me eligible to serve you in the ministry of the New Testament in the Holy Spirit through Jesus Christ our Lord, Amen.V.L Zaikima, *Ka Tla Fai Ta...* 98-99 (transcribed by the author).

608 O God our father, I am under the control of Satan, I try to escape from it, but it is not possible for me. I can not come out of my bondage since I am tied up by the cruel rope of Satan. I try many times by entering in different gospel

2.1.3. Normal Christians: They are Christian but they are neither involved in the church ministry nor commit overt sins; they are learners of a Christian life. To this group the prayer slogan[609] is mainly centred on empowering the believers to be fit for facing various temptations, hardships and to be able to live faithfully and follow the footsteps of Jesus Christ.

2.1.4. Nominal Christians: For them the prayer slogan[610] is mainly focused towards the grace of God to be upon them and also to give thanks to God as well as to set them free from the bondage of sins.

2.2. Appraisal of the Prayer Slogan

As stated, prayer slogans are taught by compulsion, but this is difficult to appreciate. It may be useful for the campers for self reflection but at the same time it can be a kind of brainwash since it is a must. Lalthuama stated, "*let the innocent campers realize that this kind of reciting the prayer slogan together like children is a means of*

camp and campaigns, but I often return to my previous status since I could not receive the victory of Calvary; but Lord I now return to you by knowing that you can forgive my sins because of your grace, I surrender and draw near to you with repentance with all my heart and confess all my sins. Lord, please cleanse me with the blood and lead me with your Holy Spirit. Amen. V. L. Zaikima, *Ka Tla Fai Ta...* 98 (transcribed by the author).

609 O, Lord! Guide and show me your suffering at Calvary, for those who ever see your love will surely praise your name. O Lord, help me to strengthen my faith and to remove my suspicion. Sanctifiers of the heart, helper of the soul rebirth, give me a new heart; make my heart more beautiful for you, through Jesus Christ our Lord, Amen. V. L. Zaikima, *Ka Tla Fai Ta...* 99. (Transcribed by the author).

610 O, God, due to the sins of Adam and Eve your wrath has been imposed even upon us till today. You have vowed that the sinners will be punished; accordingly we are to be punished. We still inherit the sins of Adam and Eve. We have been informed in the counselling class that we cannot avoid your punishment; we are very clear about your Word, now we pray and beseech you to forgive our sins. Lord, forgive us and communicate to us to know your voice through the Biblical verses or songs, we pray in Jesus name, Amen V.L Zaikima, *Ka Tla Fai Ta...* 99-100. (Transcribed by the author).

brainwash."[611] There is possibility that it is not for brainwash but to guide and to let them know how to pray to God.

The first prayer slogan needs more evaluation. The first sentence that mentions the unworthiness of the minister is acceptable, as the status of minister-ship is not to be proud of; rather it is a servanthood ministry. In some, pride might be found, but not in all ministers. If the ministry is just to please others not God then it is dangerous and it will not inspire, rather it will obliterate their spiritual life. But the group leaders do not really know the personal conviction. One of the main contents of the slogan is "Lord I have served you without receiving baptism of the Holy Spirit, and all my service was a waste of time and nothing…."[612] Here we see that 'there is a gap between the time of conversion and the Baptism of the Holy Spirit, this is not safe since the conversion of the person is the work of the Holy Spirit.'[613] This sentence also concern the sanctity of the church and its ministry, since the ministers are called by God, ordained through the church.

Campers are compelled to blame their previous ministries, calling them "*a waste of time and nothing.*" This is difficult to accept and follow; at first campers have difficulty in obeying them.[614] If they refuse to say, they are charged "as *disobedient, proud minister, not humble, and need humility,*"[615] so they must follow the dictated slogan. This teaching gives a negative attitude to the campers towards their past ministries as a waste of time and useless. The report of Study Commission ATC also expressed negative comment: "It can be heard that, there are many fruitful ministers who blame their previous ministries as a waste of time and useless, through their fresh testimonies."[616]

---

611 C. Lalthuama, *El- Bethel Camp Hla* …,12th Stanza (unpublished).

612 R. Vanlaltluanga "Revival Movements…, 34.

613 The Report of the Study Commission (Aizawl Theological College Faculty), on the Bethel Revival Movement, p. 5 (unpublished).

614 Lalhmangaiha, "A Study of the Theology …, 35.

615 C. Thansiama interviewed on 6.5.2006 at his residence. Upa Lalhluna interviewed on 12.5.2006.

616 The Report of the Study Commission (Aizawl Theological College Faculty), on the Bethel Revival Movement, 1990, 5.

Undermining the previous ministry is not safe. Before the El-Bethel Team was established, uncountable effective ministries were carried out by the wonderful and active guidance of the Holy Spirit throughout the centuries and till today. The team accuses the previous ministries of the churches that they can be charged as proud ministers, claiming that their ministry only is true, greater and recognized by God. C. Lalthuama stated, "Who is this man, blaming and rejecting the appointed ministers of the church leaders like pastors and elders, by looking down on their ministry and claiming and flattering himself superior as lover of sinners...."[617] This kind of teaching is not acceptable, since contemporary ministry is the outcome of the past ministries of the church under the guidance of the Holy Spirit.

The group leader does not know whether the ministers are appointed by the Holy Spirit or not, he cannot directly ask them to withdraw and negate their previous ministries, since they are appointed by the church committee or convention. Some might be false ministers, though they are appointed by the church; even among the disciples of Jesus a traitor was there. There can be mistakes, but this does not mean that all other disciples are traitors. The prayer slogan helps the person to reflect on himself as well as his ministries; then he will notice his weaknesses and confess his sins and slothfulness. This helps the person to pray for the fresh inspiration of the Holy Spirit and can lead him to repentance and a fresh start towards his responsibilities in the ministries.

The Bethel Prayer system works for the benefit[618] of self reflection. This system is favoured by the people and also independent preachers continue this system till today. This Bethel prayer is a turning point in Mizoram church history in relation to prayer.

In the Bethel Prayer most of the campers accepted that their prayer was answered. At the same time, Bethel Prayer clarifies that God is not confined in a particular church, and can be communicated

617 C. Lalthuama, *El- Bethel Camp Hla...*, 2nd Stanza (unpublished, translated by the author).

618 Most of the interviewees shared that they are really benefited by the Bethel Prayer.

from every corner. So, Bethel Prayer can be effective, in drawing Christians closer to God.

3. The Doctrine of the Holy Spirit

In the Teaching of K. Hminga there was no "systematic" understanding of the doctrine of the Holy Spirit. Nevertheless, it was one of the most emphasized topics through out the El-Bethel Revival movement. Vanlaltluanga stated that, "For him the Holy Spirit is the giver of Revival."[619]

The other aspect of new interest in the El-Bethel movement was that the Holy Spirit was the enlightener of their wickedness, and enlivener of their lives. They addressed the Holy Spirit as the remover of evil inclinations. John Macquarie mentioned that "the Holy Spirit then is God's coming to (human) in an inward way to enlighten and strengthen him."[620] Though the Holy Spirit is manifested as a comforter and helper of their needs, K. Hminga did not clearly understand the continual dwelling presence of the Holy Spirit. K. Hminga believed that when the Holy Sprit is with them their mental disturbance, sorrow, weariness are taken away.[621] His understanding of the Holy Spirit lacks the understanding of the permanent abiding presence of the Holy Spirit with them.

The most interesting aspect in relation to K. Hminga's understanding of the Holy Spirit is that of "baptism in the Holy Spirit." It was thought to be a second encounter with God (the first is conversion), in which the Christian begins to receive the supernatural power of the Holy Spirit into his life. K. Hminga claimed to have conversion in February 1962, and receive the baptism of Holy Spirit on 18th April, 1978 at 2 PM.[622] This perspective highlights that

619 R. Vanlaltluanga, "Revival Movement"..., 50.

620 John Macquarie, *Jesus Christ in Modern Thought* (London: SCM Press, 1990), 333.

621 K. Lalhmingliana, "Pentikaws Thlarau Thiltum" *El-Bethel Magazine* 1/6 (October, 1991), 6-8

622 K. Lalhmingliana, *El-Bethel Camp Sermon ...*, 210; *Zo Ni Eng*, Vol. V, 17-24 January 1990:5; *Autobiography of Lalhmingliana...*, 7; H. T. Kunga, "El-Bethel Camp Speaker Pu K. Lalhmingliana Hi tunge a nih?" *EL-BETHEL Magazine* 1/1 (April 1990), 4.

Christian does not receive the Holy Spirit at the time of conversion, but the baptism of the Holy Spirit is a later incident. Here we see that 'there is a gap between the time of conversion and the Baptism of the Holy Spirit. This is not safe since the conversion of the person is the work of the Holy Spirit.'[623] This teaching created the belief that one's service in the ministry of the gospel of Christ before receiving the Holy Spirit baptism was in vain and worthless.

At the same time, John Macquarie recognised four "moments" in the process of the entry of the Holy Spirit in the Christian Life. These moments are- *conviction of sin*, *repentance*, *election*, *justification*. This passes into the progressive work of sanctification, in which the Holy Spirit more and more conforms this life to Christ, deepening and extending it in faith, hope and love.[624] This Holy Spirit is given to all Christians, to lead them into the fullness of truth in Christ.[625]

4. Ministry of the Church

K. Hminga's understanding of ministry run by the church is very limited. Because of this, the theme of his Team is "**Humility: The Gospel that reaches sinners.**"[626] To him the ministry run by the churches does not properly reach the sinners and he stated that his "ministry is to liberate the CSW, drugs addicts and alcoholics who are neglected by the ministry of the church and other evangelists (independent preachers)."[627] This understanding and teaching can impress negatively on the campers to look down on the church. He also accuses the church's ministry and its people for neglecting evangelisation as well as liberative work for the sinners. He stated:

> Let us examine whether our ministry has got in touch with the sinners. There are many people who faced robbery in

623 The Report of the Study Commission (ATC Faculty) on the Bethel Revival Movement, 1990: 5.

624 John Macquarie, *Jesus Christ in Modern Thought* ..., 334.

625 John 14:26 But the Advocate, the Holy Spirit, whom the Father will send in my name, will teach you everything, and remind you of all that I have said to you (NRSV).

626 To him sinners mean CSW, alcoholics, drug addicts, illicit liquor seller and producers. *Autobiography of Lalhmingliana* ...., 32.

627 *Autobiography of Lalhmingliana* ...., 32.

> the road between Jericho to heavenly Jerusalem. Have we ever anointed oil on their wounds, the most urgent need of our country is the one who is having the Gospel that reaches sinners....our Good News has reached only the good people, but it is not enough...[628]

From the above statement we can see that there are many people who really need the Gospel in action. But there is no adequate effort on the part of the church to reach the sinners who do not attend church meetings. For this the El-Bethel team preached, worked, and cared for these people. This is one of the main challenges of the El-Bethel Team.

Though the ministry of the church may not be up to the expectation, this does not mean that the church neglects the sinners. The Presbyterian Church already takes initiative to reach these people since 1978, and introduced Synod Social Front Committee with four aims and objectives.[629] This committee distributes pamphlets to make people aware of misuse of drugs, liquor and other social evils including corruption.[630] At the same time each church takes initiative to reach the backsliders according to their convenience, but could not confine ministries only to these people. So, blaming the church's ministry towards the sinners is not right. Projecting oneself as the one who most cares for neglected people is also not right for the spirituality of the minister.

II. Conclusion

From the above discussion we can conclude that K. Hminga introduced new teachings to the Mizo Christians which were

628 K. Lalhmingliana, "Humility: The Gospel that Reaches Sinners," *El-Bethel* 1/1 (April, 1990), 9.

629 1. To teach and lead the members of the church according to the will of God from the field of politics, economics and social life. 2. To help the people to be good citizens of the states. 3. To teach for the better integration of Christianity and culture of the society 4. To work towards relief and rehabilitation with CASA and World Vision. *Mizoram Presbyterian Kohhran Department Chanchin...*, 184.

630 *Mizoram Presbyterian Kohhran Department Chanchin...*, 185.

unknown before, especially the practice of Seeds of Faith and Bethel Prayer. These new teachings are very effective and favoured by the people; it looks appropriate for the church and for ministry, but as stated the church needs to study this theology for the future ministry.

The Church needs to teach the people a sound theology which will guide them for the positive attitude of the church in relation to the doctrine of Holy Spirit as well as the ministry of the church to those outside the church. The creativity, commitment and thoughtfulness of K. Hminga enriched the church and helped the church move forward.

Chapter 6

The Analysis of the Questionnaire, Findings, Hypothesis Tested, and Final Conclusion

I. Introduction

Having described the sermons and analysis as well as the homiletical structure along with their theology in the previous chapter, in this chapter the campers as well as the church members of the Study areas' response to questionnaire is analyzed. The main intention of this is to bring out the nature, response, theology and effectiveness of the sermons of K. Hminga to the people of the church and society.

To make it more comprehensive the analysis is divided into 6 sections. The first section is the demographic details of the respondents, followed by the respondent's involvement in different Church activities. The respondent's attitudes to the El-Bethel Team are analyzed and are followed by the analysis of the respondent's attitudes of the preaching of K. Hminga in the Camp. The analysis of the respondent's opinion on the relationship of the El-Bethel ministry and the church follows. Lastly it is followed by the respondents' opinions about the contribution of the El-Bethel ministry to the society. At the end of each section an evaluation is made to highlight the findings of the whole section.

In the last section, the major findings are discussed and tested with the hypothesis of this research and final conclusion follows.

1. The Analysis of the Questionnaire

1.1. Demographic Details of the Respondents

The data for the following analysis were obtained through a Questionnaire. The Questionnaire was distributed to 70 Church members from Chanmari and Dawrpui Vengthar pastorates of Mizoram Presbyterian Church, who hold different positions in the different local Churches. Of the 70 questionnaires distributed 57 were returned, from which the following analyses were made.

1.1.1 Respondents' Gender: The respondents comprised of 57 persons, out of which 35 were male and the other 22 were female, a good proportion. It is remarkable that females represent almost half of the respondents. This would neutralize the findings from male dominated opinions for the Mizos still follow a patriarchal system in the Church ministry.

1.1.2. Marital status: 46 respondents are married and 11 respondents unmarried. It must be noted that the unmarried respondents are active youth participants in Church activities.

1.1.3. Pastorate: 25 respondents are from Chanmari pastorate, 32 respondents are from Dawrpui Vengthar pastorates. This also indicates that the proportion of the respondents is not too different to one another.

1.1.4. Age group: Table showing the respondents' age group: It is classified into 4 categories.

Sl. No	Age Group	No. respondents	Percentage
1	66 years above	8	14%
2	46-65 years	27	47%
3	26-45 years	21	36%
4	25 below	1	1.7%
5	Total	57	

This table indicates that the majority is from 46 to 65, they are 27 (47%) respondents and the second is 26 to 45, they are 21 (36%) respondents. This shows that mostly the campers were middle aged while El-Bethel camp was organized in 1990 (16 years ago). The numbers of respondents from the different age groups are: only 1 respondent from the age group of 25 and below; from 66 and above there are 8 respondents.

1.1.5. Status in the Family: Regarding the respondents' status in the family, there are 29 fathers, 21 mothers, 5 sons, and 2 daughters.

1.1.6. Occupation: Respondents are classified into 7 categories on the basis of their occupation. 27 respondents are Govt. employees. Next are the self-employed such as business people, making up 16 respondents. The other respondents consist of 1 Farmer, 1 Cultivator, 5 Manual labourers, and 7 respondents are dependants.

1.1.7. Educational Qualifications: Regarding the respondents' educational qualifications, the largest group of 25 are graduates and above. Next are 19 High school dropouts. The third group is 13 HSLC holders.

1.1.8. Annual Income: 29 (50%) of the respondents have an income above Rs. 1, 00, 000/- annually. 18 (31%) respondents have an income more than 50,000/- annually. Those who are in these groups have a stable income from government jobs and businesses. The other 8 respondents whose annual incomes do not cross Rs. 50000/- are manual labourers; students and other who are dependants on other family member may also be included in this group.

Evaluation of the Demographic Details of the Respondents: From the demographic detail of the respondents, we have a good proportion of male and female, married and unmarried[631] and of respondents from the two pastorates. Regarding the participation of different age groups, the majority 47% age group is 46-65. At the same time, the participation from the younger groups (36%) and

631 Though the number of unmarried respondents is less in the overall participation, for this research, having 11 unmarried respondents may be regarded as good participation. In the context of Mizo Christians all unmarried active members of the church, except for a few exceptional cases, are active members of the Youth department.

the older groups (14%) to counteract the possibility of any bias is satisfactory.

Regarding the occupation, educational qualifications and annual income of the respondents, there is a satisfactory representation of respondents that represent all positions in the society though the majorities are from affluent background. Therefore, it may be concluded that the respondents for this research have been proportionately represented to obtain a fair idea of camper's attitude towards the preaching and results in the El-Bethel Camp.

1.2. Respondents' Status and Involvement in Church Activities

1.2.1. Status in the Church: Among the respondents there are 12 ordained people, 1 Pastor and 11 Elders. 13 respondents (22%) are Office bearers and committee members of Youth and Women in the Church. Besides 25 respondents (43%) are the ones who hold different posts in the local church ministry.[632] The remaining 7 respondents are active Church members.

1.2.2. Attendance of Church Service: Since the majority of the respondents are those who hold important responsibilities in the church, it is not surprising that the campers in the El-Bethel camp are regular Churchgoers. 26 (45%) respondents attended all church services 5 times in a week; 22 (38%) respondents attended services 4 times a week, another 6 attended services 3 times, 1 attended services only once in a week.

1.2.3. Involvement in Church Activities: Respondents are mostly active in Church activities other than regular worship services and official meetings at the level of local church, especially in voluntary work. In the context of Churches in Mizoram, almost all necessary works are done by the members voluntarily. Since none can participate regularly in all voluntary works, occasional involvement may be taken to mean regular involvement.

1.2.4. Wider Church Activities: Majority of the respondents are occasionally involved in activities other than in their local churches. Only 17 respondents, i.e. 29% are regularly involved at the

632 They are preachers, Teachers in the Sunday school, various sub., Committee members.

Pastorate, Presbytery and Synod level, and 28 (49%) respondents are occasionally involved in the pastorate, Presbytery and Synod level. Only 6 (10%) are never involved at this level.

Evaluation of Respondents' Status and Involvement in Church activities: This section reveals the status of the respondents in the church and their involvement in church activities. Only 7 respondents (12%) are ordinary members in the church. All the other 50 respondents (88%) are leaders and those who hold important responsibilities at least at the local level. This proportionate imbalance of respondents between leaders of the church and active members may have affected the findings in favour of the preaching in the El-Bethel camp. In a Mizo fundamentalist Christian mind set, making a critical yet positive comment on Church activities is generally not expected from those who hold important responsibilities in the Church.

1.3. The Respondents' Attitudes to the El-Bethel Team

1.3.1. Table Showing the Familiarity of the El-Bethel Team to the People

S. No.	How did you know the El-Bethel Team?	No. Respondents	Percentage
1	From Friends/ families	16	28%
2	From media *e.g.* news paper, T. v. etc.	11	19%
3	From the church announcement	30	52%
5	Total	57	

The above table shows that the popularity of El-Bethel Team was vast; even before people attended the El-Bethel camp: 57 respondents (100%) had already heard through the above communications, the church announcement was the main.

1.3.2. Personal Experience of the El-Bethel Camp: 49 respondents (85%) were campers in the El-Bethel camp and 8 respondents (14%) did not enter in the El-Bethel camp. This shows that the sources are reliable enough for the purpose.

1.3.3. Reasons for entering in the El-Bethel Camp: 47 respondents (82%) entered the El-Bethel camp because of personal willingness, 5 respondents (8%) each entered the camp by family pressure or due to the invitation of peer groups.

3.4. Table showing Campers' Attitudes to the El-Bethel Camp

S. No.	What is your attitude to El-Bethel camp?	No. Respondents	Percentage
1	Very good	47	82.45%
2	Boring	-	
3	Interesting	10	17.54%
4	Not good	-	
5	No idea	-	
	Total	57	100%

The above table shows that all campers are having positive attitude; they liked and enjoyed the camp. No campers have negative attitude against the El-Bethel camp.

Evaluation of Respondents' Attitudes to the El-Bethel Camp: This section reveals that El-Bethel team was popular and most of the ministers and members of the churches are very much attracted by the El-Bethel team's ministry. People are thirsty for the word of God and to quench their thirst through their personal willingness they entered the Camp. El-Bethel camp was really good and interesting for them.

1.4. The Respondents' Attitudes to the Preaching in the Camp

1.4.1. Table showing the Respondents' Attitudes about the Preaching of K. Hminga

S. No.	Do you think that Mr. K. Hminga was a good preacher?	No. Respondents	Percentage
1	Very good	17	29.82%
2	Good	38	66.66%
3	Normal	2	3.50%
4	Not good	-	
5	Total	57	

This table clearly reveals that all the respondents favour the preaching of K. Hminga.

Regarding his articulation 26 respondents (45%) says that the preacher is '*very good*,' 20 respondents (35%) say that he is '*good*' and 10 respondents (17%) say that he is '*excellent*' in articulation. This result highlighted that the preacher is really good in articulation.

1.4.2. Respondents' Attitudes about the Main Theme and Focus of the Speaker in his Preaching: According to most of the respondents the main theme and focus of the speaker in his preaching is: *The gospel that reaches sinners*; 46 respondents (80%) choose it. This shows that the speaker is successful in the preaching ministry, since the main theme of the team is clearly presented through preaching.

1.4.3. The Spiritual Benefits of the Respondents of the El-Bethel Camp: 44 respondents (77%) says that they 'benefited' from the camp, 13 respondents (22%) say that they are 'very much benefited' by the camp. This shows that 99% of the campers say that camp is supportive for their spiritual life.

1.4.4. The Respondents' Attitudes on the Attractiveness of the Preaching: This section reveals that 42 respondents (73%) say that the preaching was '*very attractive*' and 14 respondents (24%) say that it was '*attractive*' and only 3% say that the preaching was *not attractive*. This reveals that the preaching was mostly attractive to the people. The reasons of the attractiveness of preaching highlighted by the respondents are the following: First, because of his serious commitment (61%); secondly, because his preaching is very interesting (30%); thirdly because of the unceasing prayer for him (9%) by the Tawngtai Khawl and the church members; this is directly related to the work of the Holy Spirit.

1.4.5. The Respondents' Attitudes on the Theology of K. Hminga: All the respondents including pastor and elders say that the teaching and theology of K. Hminga for the church is safe. There are 29 respondents (50%) who want to continue the *Seeds of Faith* practice and there are 21 respondents (36%) who want to stop the Seeds of faith practice in the future ministry of the church. 7 respondents (12%) could not give proper answers. This shows that the Seeds of Faith practice is mostly accepted by the respondents but many respondents are disturbed by this teaching. As some are against the Seeds of Faith practice, it is questionable how they can say all the theological teachings are safe, this shows that they do not evaluate the Seeds of Faith critically.

1.4.6. The Respondent's Attitudes about whether the El-Bethel Sermons are Biblically Grounded: There are 47 respondents (82%) in the side that 'the El-Bethel sermons are Biblically grounded.' Meanwhile there are four respondents (7%) who are against this opinion; the other six respondents (10%) do not give their opinion.

1.4.7. The Respondents' Attitudes about the Clarity of the Sermons of K. Hminga: 42 respondents (73%) say that the sermon was '*clear and easy to understand*' and 8 respondents (14%) say that it was '*very clear*,' but the other 8 respondents (14%) say that it was '*partly clear but not all sermons*.'

All the respondents favour the sermons of K. Hminga. The reasons are ranked accordingly by the following: 1. It is inclusive (31% respondents choose it); 2 His thorough physical and spiritual preparation for the sermon (28% respondents choose it); 3. He preaches through his practical experiences (22% respondents choose it); 4. The relevancy of the messages (19% respondents choose it)

1.4.8. The Respondent's Attitudes about the Illustrations and Gestures of the Preacher: This section clearly reveals that all the respondents found the illustrations in the sermons are supportive to the message. Regarding his expressions and gestures 50 respondents (87%) say that it was appropriate with the preaching, the rest (13%) do not have idea in this regard.

1.4.9. The Respondent's Attitudes about Uniqueness of the Preaching of K. Hminga: 33 respondents (57%) say that the preaching of K. Hminga was different from the preaching of others, 10 respondents (17%) say that there is no uniqueness in his preaching, and 5 respondents (8%) do not have idea about it. The reasons for uniqueness are ranked according to the percentage: 1. He preaches what he has experiences (42%); 2. His sermon structure is simple and easy to remember (38%); 3. He was efficient in using illustrations (31%); 4. His sermons are shorter than other sermons (36%).

Evaluation of Respondents' Attitudes to the Preaching in the El-Bethel Camp: This section reveals that the preaching in the camp was good; attractive, clear and easy to understand and very much favoured by the respondents; the preacher is talented in articulation. The El-Bethel sermons are Biblically grounded and the illustrations in the sermons are supportive and gestures are pertinent. The speaker is successful in the preaching ministry; this can be identified that his main purpose is clearly presented and received by the audience, and it benefited most of the campers. His enormous commitment seems to be the most reasonable for the success of his preaching. And he is accepted as a well-known preacher for his time.

All respondents agree that his theology is safe for the church, but as we have discussed, the theology in relation to the *Seeds of Faith* and *Bethel Prayer* is an issue about which the church needs to be careful. Regarding K. Hminga's uniqueness in preaching, K. Hminga preaches his experiences. He regularly repeats the same sermons which will surely help the smooth presentation, articulation, use of illustrations, clarity of the message, application and appropriateness of the messages. It is difficult to criticise since the same sermons are often preached lively and received lively by the audience. This shows that beyond the content of sermon there is an inspiration of the Holy Sprit in the preaching, which is immeasurable. In El-Bethel revival movement preaching was the main event, this is the distinction of El-Bethel revival from the rest of others revival in Mizoram.

1.5. The Respondents Attitudes to El-Bethel Ministry and the Church

1.5.1. Table Showing the Respondents' Attitudes to the Ministry in Relation to Interpersonal Relationship among the members of the church

S. No.	Do you agree that the ministry of El-Bethel enhance interpersonal relationship in the church?	No. Respondents	Percentage
1	Strongly Agree	11	19.29%
2	Agree	43	75.43%
3	Not agree	3	5.26%
4	Total	57	

This section reveals that 94.72% *agree* that El-Bethel preaching ministry enhances interpersonal relationships among the members of the church.

1.5.2. The respondents' attitudes to; whether due to K. Hminga's preaching people pay less attention to the Preaching of the Pastors and Elders: 52 respondents (91%) disagreed that due to the preaching of K. Hminga people pay less attention to the preaching of the pastors and elders. At the same time 3 respondents (5%) agreed this attitude.

1.5.3. The respondents' attitudes to the result of the El-Bethel Team's ministry in relation to the increase of the Church members: This section reveals that 51 respondents (89%) *agreed* that due to the El-Bethel Team's ministry the numbers of the church members increased, but 6 respondents (10%) disagreed with this opinion.

1.5.4. The respondents' attitudes to the results of the El-bethel Team in relation to the upliftment of the Church: 52 respondents (91%) accept that the El-Bethel Team's ministry *uplifts* the ministry of the church, and 4 respondents (7%) also agreed that it *partly uplifts,* while only one respondent is against this thought. The following ranks are given by the respondents in the area of its upliftment:

1. It increased the offerings of the church.
2. It increased the members of the church
3. It gave awareness to the churches to care for the poor and backsliders
4. It helped the worship service to become lively
5. It aroused the members in the church activity

Especially in relation to the rise of offerings, 48 respondents (84%) strongly accept that it was due to the ministry of El-Bethel team; at the same time 9 respondents (15%) can not say the exact real cause.

1.5.5. The respondents' attitudes whether El-Bethel Ministry is a burden for the Church or not: 40 respondents (70%) agree that El-Bethel camp ministry is not a burden for the church but 15 respondents (26%) disagree with the above thought; this shows that Bethel Camp was helpful for the church but to some extent it was a burden for the church, since it takes time, money, hard work.

1.5.6. The respondents' attitudes whether there is something to learn about his preaching for the Pastors and Elders: 53 respondents (92%) agree that there is something to learn about the preaching of K. Hminga for the Pastors and Elders, while 2 respondents (3%) did not see any thing for the Pastors and Elders to learn, other 2 respondents (3%) did not give their idea.

This shows that there is something to learn for the Pastors and Elders. The following ranks are given by the respondents of things to learn by the Pastors and Elders from the preaching of K. Lalhmingliana:

1) Seriousness while delivering sermon
2) Mastering the text and content of the sermon
3) Using relevant and practical experiences in the sermon illustration
4) Completion of sermon within 25-30 minutes

Evaluations of Respondents' Attitudes to El-Bethel Ministry and the Church: From the response, it is made known that El-Bethel preaching ministry enhances interpersonal relationships among the members of the church. People do not hesitate to listen to the preaching of the Pastors and Elders, even after listening to the preaching of K. Hminga. The Team's ministry helped the church members to increase and respondent find that there is something new to learn for the Pastors and Elders in the preaching of K. Hminga. In every preaching there is something to learn; this does not mean that pastors and elders are not effective preachers, since people do not hesitate to listen to their preaching.

1.6. The Respondents' Attitudes to the Influence of El-Bethel Ministry on Society

1.6.1. The respondents' attitudes on the restoration of families in the El-Bethel ministry: This section clearly reveals that the 31 respondents (54%) '*Accepted*' and 21 respondents (36%) '*Strongly accepted*' that the preaching ministry of El-Bethel Team restores many families in a better Christian family, while 5 respondents (8%) accepted partly; this shows that no respondents are against the idea.

1.6.2. The respondents' attitudes to the role of El-Bethel Team in relation to inter-relationship among the churches: 48 respondents (84%) *accepted* and 5 respondents (8%) *strongly accepted* that there is a better relationship among the different denominations due to the ministry of the El-Bethel team; at the same time there are 5 respondents (8%) who do not accept this matter.

1.6.3. The respondents' attitudes to about the reformation of social life by the El-Bethel revival movement: 41 respondents (71%) accept that the El-Bethel revival movement '*reforms*' the social life of the society, and 16 respondents (28%) accept that this El-Bethel Revival movement '*partly reforms*' the social life of the society, no respondent oppose that the El-Bethel revival movement reforms the social life of the society. So this section clearly reveals that El-Bethel team contributes enormously for the reformation of the society.

1.6.4. The respondents' attitudes about the contributions of the El-Bethel Team in the Society: 41 respondents (71%) agree that due to the El-Bethel revival movement integration in the society the gap between the rich and the poor is reduced not financially, there is less discrimination, social relationships are integrated. 24 respondents (42%) accept that El-Bethel movement teaches to be faithful in each individual profession; this can be indirectly related to corruption, negligence of duties etc. This shows that El-Bethel movement was very significant, and acceptable to the society.

1.6.5. The respondents' attitudes about the weaknesses of the El-Bethel Team: The respondents are fair enough to reveal weaknesses. The following major points are ranked accordingly as the weaknesses of the El-Bethel Team:

1) There was no systematic administration in the Team (33%)
2) The counsellors are too young and less experienced (26%)
3) There is no exact relationship of the organizer church with El-Bethel Team (15%)
4) They do not have fresh sermons but are repeated many times (10%)

This shows that even though they are very successful in preaching ministry, they also faced problems in their administration.

Evaluations of Respondents' Attitudes to the Influence of El-Bethel Ministry on Society: This reveals that the preaching ministry of El-Bethel Team restores many families in a better Christian family. There is better relationship among the different denominations due to the ministry of the El-Bethel team; it is also clear that El-Bethel revival movement reforms and integrates the social relationship in the society. Meanwhile there is a weakness in the team too in the maintenance of relationship with the camp organizer churches.

2. Major Findings from the Analysis of the Questionnaire

From what has been analyzed so far in this chapter, the following are the major findings:

1. El-Bethel Team's ministry is popular and attractive to the **people:** Most of the members of the churches said that they are familiar with El-Bethel team and are very much attracted; most of the members enter the El-Bethel camp, most of them are entering by their personal willingness. At the same time 91% likes El-Bethel

camp. This reveals that El-Bethel team is popular and attractive to the people.

2. People favour the Preaching of K. Hminga: 61% says that the reason is because of his serious commitment in his ministry, and interesting to 95% of the respondents. (Interesting includes articulation, illustrations, expressions and gestures). It is also unique. The following points are accepted as the uniqueness. 1. He mainly preaches only what he has experienced. 2. His sermon structure is simple and easy to remember. 3. He was efficient in using illustrations. 4. His sermons are shorter than the other sermons.

Meanwhile there is no single point for the attractiveness of the preaching of K. Hminga. 31% respondents consider 'inclusiveness' as the reason of attractiveness, 28% say that it is due to the 'thorough physical and spiritual preparation' of the sermon and 22% say that it is through 'his practical experiences.' This finding indicates that it is difficult to have a convincing conclusion since the percentage is shared. Besides the combination of the above three reasons covers 81% of the whole idea, so the above points can be accepted as the reasons of attractiveness.

3. People do not hesitate to listen the Preaching of the Pastors and Elders, as a result of the Preaching of K. Hminga: Many people flock to the camp of El-Bethel Team; they were revived and return to the church with fresh joy. 91% accept that due to the preaching of K. Hminga people do not hesitate to listen to the preaching of the pastors and elders of their own churches.

4. El-Bethel Team's ministry uplifts the ministry of the Church: It is convincing that the ministry of El-Bethel team uplifts the ministry of the churches. The following are the main areas:

1) It increases the offerings of the church.
2) It increases the members of the church.
3) It raises awareness of the churches to care for the poor and backsliders.

5. There is something to learn for the Pastors and Elders from the preaching of K. Hminga: This finding reveals that there is some thing to learn for the pastors and elders. The following ranks are given by the respondents.

1) Seriousness while delivering sermon.
2) Mastering the text and content of the sermon.
3) Using relevant and practical life experiences in the sermon illustrations.
4) Completion of sermon within 25-30 minutes.

6. The Preaching Ministry of El-Bethel Team restores many families in a better Christian family: This finding shows that the El-Bethel ministry was really helpful for the restoration of Christian family in the field of husband-wife relationship and new introduction of regular family devotion in some families.

7. There is better inter-relationship among the various Churches due to the ministry of El-Bethel Team: When El-Bethel camp is organized there is no boundary for a single church or denomination; people did not care about their denomination; El-Bethel camp pulled all the churches together under the umbrella of El-Bethel Team, i. e. Inter-denominational.

8. K. Hminga introduced new teachings to the Mizo Christians which were especially the practice of Seeds of Faith and Bethel Prayer. These new teachings are very effective and favoured by the people; it looks appropriate for the church and for ministry, but as stated the church needs to study his teaching for better result in the life and ministry of the church.

9. The creativity, commitment and thoughtfulness of K. Hminga and his Team enriched the church and helped the church move forward for the extension of the Kingdom of God.

3. Summary of the Major Findings

1. K. Hminga's serious commitment is the reason for the attractiveness of his preaching.
2. There is uniqueness in the preaching of K. Hminga.
3. People did not reject the preaching of the Pastors and Elders, as a result of the preaching of K. Hminga.
4. There is something to learn from the Evangelical type of preaching from K. Hminga for the Pastors and Elders.
5. The preaching ministry of El-Bethel Team restores many families in a better Christian family.

6. There are better relationships among the churches due to the ministry of El-Bethel Team.
7. There is certainly fresh anointing of the blessed God the Holy Spirit every time he stands to preach, even if he repeats the sermon.
8. God chose him to use him to bring revival in spite of his lack of education and weaknesses or limitations in his team. (E.g. immature prayer leaders, no expository preaching, etc.)
9. The indigenous evangelical homiletic structure is simple Topical by structure. In relation the form and content directly it is a mixture of testimonial end experiential. This requires deep and hard practical labour in life. Delivery with the skill of indigenous rhetorical passion to grab and convince the audience with the help of the Holy Spirit.

4. Final Conclusion

4.1. Hypotheses Tested: As has been noted in INTRODUCTION: V. 5, a number of hypotheses were formulated. These hypotheses are tested as follows:

4.1.1. Hypothesis: The Preaching of Revival Preachers is more attractive than that of the Pastors and Elders of the Presbyterian Church: This hypothesis is proved to be true because more than half of the people (73%) are more attracted to and interested in the preaching of the Evangelical preacher than the preaching of the pastors and elders of the Presbyterian Church. However, people do not abandon listening to the preaching of the Pastors and Elders, as a result of the preaching of K. Hminga. Many people flock to the camp of El-Bethel Team for an appointed time for a special purpose; they are revived and return to the church with fresh joy under the ministry of the same pastor and elders.

4.1.2. Hypothesis: The El-Bethel Sermons are not Biblically grounded: This hypothesis is proved to be wrong since 82% of the respondents accept that the sermons of the El-Bethel Team are Biblically grounded. So, it is reliable to accept that the El-Bethel preaching is Biblically grounded and theologically sound.

4.1.3. Hypothesis: There is no sufficient Exposition of the Texts in the El-Bethel Preaching. This hypothesis is proved to be true. This is not asked in the questionnaire because it is related to technical studies since most of the respondents are lay people; but it is confirmed through the analysis of the sermons of K. Lalhmingliana. The analysis of five sermons of K. Hminga reveals that the sermons really lack exposition of the Biblical references. His sermons are not expository, and are more topical in type. This is the weakness of K. Hminga in his preaching. But on the other hand this is the Evangelical homiletic by nature. There is no big space for biblical exposition in the evangelical type of preaching.

4.1.4. Hypothesis: The El-Bethel Evangelical preaching increases the collections of the Church offerings: This hypothesis is proven as correct. To know the exact growth rate of the offerings of the churches, see Appendix No.4.

4.2. The Lessons that the Church Can Learn

4.2.1. Members of the Churches are very attracted by the Independent preachers: Church members are very attracted by the preaching ministry of K. Hminga; some of the reasons have been already stated. This shows that the conventional practice of preaching in the church is not adequate to feed the spiritual needs of the members. So the preachers in the churches must update their preaching in various ways.

4.2.2. The Elders and Pastors of the Church need to improve their Preaching: As has been mentioned in the findings, the elders and the pastors need to learn five important points through the preaching of K. Hminga for the better result of their preaching.

1. Seriousness while delivering sermon
2. Mastering the text and content of the sermon
3. Using relevant and practical life experiences in the sermon illustration.
4. Completions of sermon within 25-30 minutes; since the capacity of the people is reduced and also they are engaged in various other programmes.

5. Proper exposition of the text should be practiced by the elders and pastors in their sermon preparation and delivery (Which was lacking in the preaching of K. Hminga).

The above points and proposals highlighted that the elders and pastors need to be serious in their sermon preparation as well as delivering the messages from the pulpit. To attain such seriousness the elders and pastors need to know and experience the burden and responsibility of the preacher.

Mastering the texts and contents of the sermons need thorough study, demand sufficient preparation and practices even before delivery of the sermon from the pulpit and to be able to include relevant illustrations, regular collection from books, experiences and others must be carried out. Then it will be a great benefit for the congregation as well as for the preachers.

4.2.3. The Church must regularly update its ministry to meet the need of the spiritual life of the people: As stated in the summary of the major findings the preaching ministry of El-Bethel Team restored many broken families to a better Christian family. The Church must constantly study the condition and problems of the members' families to be able to provide and nurture its members for the growth of their spiritual life. The ministry of K. Hminga reveals that there are many Christians who are not living as they ought. This shows that the church needs to update and widen its ministry to bring the backsliders back to the church. Inviting people like K. Hminga or other Evangelistic teams may be helpful. Therefore, the church must learn how to give them spiritual food through the regular preaching of the elders and pastors.

4.2.4 Preaching and Practise must go hand in hand: One of the attractiveness of the evangelical preaching of K. Hminga was that, his preaching was applied by him practically. Saying and delivering big words and interesting sermons are not enough to draw and convince the people. So the preachers of the church must learn and apply what they preach. People observe the life of the preacher; not only do they pay attention to their preaching but also their family, spiritual life and social behaviour. Guidance and advice can be given to the elders and pastors from this.

4.2.5 Independent Preachers and Revival Movement need proper care: Unlike the other revival movements in North East India as shown in the Major Findings number 4, the El-Bethel revival movement through Evangelical homiletic increases the members of the church than losing them. This shows that caring and steering the revival preachers and their teams in the revival movement is really helpful for the growth of the church members, so the church must learn thoroughly how to collaborate and handle Evangelical preacher as well as their team by the church leaders.

Since the main speaker of the El-Bethel Team K. Hminga has already died, it has not been possible to reorganize the team, but there are many other independent preachers in India and abroad. The church must learn how to cooperate and make use of these committed preachers and must be ready for the future ministry and prepare herself through this experience.

4.2.6. The Church must organize Homiletical Training Programme for the Independent Preacher for better Biblical Preaching: As it is shown in the analysis of the sermons of K .Hminga there is no proper exposition of the Texts. The independent preachers need some basic knowledge of homiletics skills. For this, the church can organize special Homiletical Training Programme for the itinerant and independent preachers as well as for the lay leaders of the church; this will promote their preaching for better result.

4.3. Significance for Today

4.3.1. K. Hminga's life and Evangelical homiletic type continue to be relevant in the context of a growing number of independent preachers in India and abroad. Many independent preachers have come and gone. Some begun with great enthusiasm but fell on account of various reasons. But K .Hminga was the one who remained faithful to his call and commitment to the end. He never went out of the church nor spoke against it nor preached prosperity gospel. He never contemplated on starting a new denomination. He preached what he himself practised and practised what he preached. He remains an attested example to all independent preachers among the indigenous Indian preachers.

4.3.2. As fascinating religious personality he combined in himself a desire for freedom from all controls including that of the ecclesiastical authority on one hand and sincere obedience to the church in all its aspects of faith and practice on the other. He was an independent preacher but worked hand in hand with the church.

4.3.3. This analytical study on the preaching of K. Lalhmingliana, as an example of an Evangelical preacher shows us that as an itinerant and independent preacher, the primary concern in his life was reaching the sinners through humility. For this, experience of the baptism of Holy Spirit had a central place in his preaching. To him there should be a sound relationship between the preacher and the Holy Spirit. If the preachers are anointed by the Holy Spirit, preaching become successful, effective and powerful, for this he was very regular in prayer and personal devotion.

4.3.4. His homiletical exposition is from himself, truly native and indigenous. He was deeply religious and creative and had practical personality with a high sense of imagination. He was a fearless and forthright preacher, such kind of preachers are the need of the present society in India.

4.3.5. The aim of his Evangelical Preaching was to call for revival of spiritual life to be able to love the sinners as Jesus did. He looked into the weaknesses of his hearers and gave his life as an example of what he was saying, namely calling for humility, and love of sinners at the same time. For this the El-Bethel team preached, worked, and cared for these people. This is one of the main challenges of the El-Bethel Team.

4.3.6. As an independent preacher K. Hminga crossed the boundaries of all denominations, joining in full communion and fellowship with all denominations. Wherever he went he strengthened ecumenical attitude and he was a kind of bridge builder between interdenominational groups.

4.3.7. K. Hminga, though a great evangelical preacher, overlooked the exegesis of the Biblical text of his sermons. He was thoroughly one-sided as he preached the spiritual life, social and Christian family life. His major theological concern was neither the living Christ nor the theology of Holy Spirit; but the dynamic role and functions of the true Christians for liberation of the poor and sinners.

4.3.8. He was one of the most effective communicators of the Gospel through pictures, images and illustrations among the Modern preachers today. Without having a proper homiletic training he always spoke in conversational form and in short sentences. His language of illustration and his style of preaching are exemplary.

4.3.9. K. Hminga made use of the immature people like newly converts of: drug addicts, alcoholics and commercial sex workers effectively in his ministry as Jesus made use of the tax collectors, lepers, Samaritan women and demon possessed persons after they recovered. This is exemplary and challenging for the modern churches and ministers.

4.3.10. In the context of growing secularisation of the Christians and churches, K. Hminga's call for spiritual renewal is important. Churches not only in North East but also entire India and the world are becoming more secular. The process of secularisation is taking deep roots in India. Predominantly in the context of secularisation, his call for, life of prayer and humble witnessing of the salvific power of the Gospel of Christ is valid for all kinds of people. So the gospel must be witnessed humbly and preached with this evangelical type of preaching to the sinners as a guiding principle emphasized by this indigenous preacher of the Gospel of Christ.

Bibliography

Journals

"Bethel Camp ah Drugs man ani" *Lentlang* 11/11 (March 27, 1990): 4-5.

"Bethel Camp Thlipui in a nuai," *Sakeibaknei* 1/283 (February 16, 1990): 10.

"Bethel leh Sorkar office te." *Sakeibaknei* 1/284 (February 20, 1990): 9.

"Bethel na ah an Nu lam vangin an inthen." *Forum* 1/9 (March-April 27-3, 1990): 3.

"Bethel Thunawi." *El-Bethel Magazine* 2/14 (June, 1991): 14.

Biakhmingthanga, R. "Manipur rama El-Bethel Rawngbawlna kalzel." *El-Bethel Magazine* 5/48 (April, 1994): 16-18.

Biakhmingthanga, R. "unique election at Jalaphet-ah Inthlanna Dangdai neih ani." *El-Bethel Magazine* 6/51 (July, 1994): 15-16.

"El- Bethel Camp Mualpui leh Chite ami Zawhfel anileh ta." *Forum* 1/ 4 (February 20-27. 1990): 5.

"El-Bethel Speaker at Central Jail."*Forum* 1/12 (April, 1990): 5.

"El-Bethel Vangin Mizoram Sorkhar Kalphung abuai." *Lentlang Weekly News* 2/4 (February 16-22, 1990): 8.

Haolai, Rev. Avum. "Songpijang leh Changpijang." *El-Bethel Magazine* 7/63 (July, 1995): 12-14.

"Harhna Aizawl Khawpui leh Mizoram ah (Revival at Aizawl, Mizoram) " *Didakhe* 19/1 (January-February, 1990): 25.

Harhna XVI/ 43 (February, 1990): 1.

Harhna, XVI/50 (September 5. 1990): 2.

Khojol, Ngurtinkhum. "Testimony." *El-Bethel Magazine* 7/63 (July, 1995): 10-11.

Kunga, H. T. "El-Bethel Camp Speaker Pu K. Lalhmingliana Hi tunge a nih?" Who is K.lalhmingliana *El-Bethel Magazine* 1/1 (April, 1990): 4.

Lalhmangaiha, C. "El-Bethel at Central Jail." *El-Bethel Magazine* 1/1 (April, 1990): 2.

Lalhmingliana K. "Tlawmna nun-Misualte hnen thlengphak Chanchin Tha." *El-Bethel Magazine* 1/ I (April, 1990): 9-12.

.... "Khawvel Tukverh." *El-Bethel Magazine*1/2 (May, 1990): 3-7.

........."Taitea tel lovin." *El-Bethel Magazine* 1/3 (June, 1990): 2-8.

........"Tuihna Kang Ngailo Nun." *El-Bethel Magazine* 1/4 (July, 1990): 3-13.

..........."Thlamuanna duh lo nun." *El-Bethel Magazine* 1/6 (September, 1990): 2-7.

..........."Kros Hmelma." *El-Bethel Magazine*1/7 (October, 1990): 2-6.

..........."Puan In zauh."*El-Bethel Magazine* 1/8 (November, 1990): 2-8.

..........."Remna Lal." *El-Bethel Magazine* 1/9 (December, 1990): 2-7.

.........."Mitinin an Chhiara chu." *El-Bethel Magazine* 2/11 (February, 1991): 2-11.

.........."Kraws Fate Kalkawng." *El-Bethel Magazine* 2/12 (March & April, 1991): 2-9.

..........."Kristian Nun: Boralna Chihnih." *El-Bethel Magazine* 2/13 (May, 1991): 2-6.

.... "Counselling Kohhran." *El-Bethel Magazine* 2/14 (June, 1991): 4 -14.

.........."Kros Pathian Thiltihtheihlohna." *El-Bethel Magazine* 2/15 (July, 1991): 2-7.

.........."Pathian Ruai Ropui." *El-Bethel Magazine* 2/16 (August, 1991): 4-10.

..........."Tinungtu Thlarau Thianghlim." *El-Bethel Magazine* 2/17 (Sept., 1991): 2-7.

.........."Penticost Thlarau Thiltum." *El-Bethel Magazine* 2/18 (October, 1991): 2-8.

.... "Saltang nun." *El-Bethel Magazine* 2/19 (November, 1991): 1-5.

.........."I Ram lo Thleng Rawh se." *El-Bethel Magazine* 2/19 (Nov., 1991): 6-10.

..........."A Lokal lehna." *El-Bethel Magazine* 2/20 (December, 1991): 2-10.

.........."Tibotu Thinlung na." *El-Bethel Magazine* 3/21 (January, 1992): 2-6.

............"Mupui ang Kohhran Thianghlim."*El-Bethel Magazine* 3/22 (Feb., 1992): 2-6.

.........."Khandaih hriam tawn." *El-Bethel Magazine* 3/23 (March, 1992): 5-10.

.........."Pathian Indona." *El-Bethel Magazine* 3/23 (March, 1992): 10-14.

.........."Pathian Thuawih." *El-Bethel Magazine* 3/24 (April, 1992): 6-11.

.........."Tho ila, Bethel-ah I kal ang u." *El-Bethel Magazine* 3/25 (May, 1992): 2-7.

.........."Krista a Kan Nihna." *El-Bethel Magazine* 3/25 (May, 1992): 8-12.

.........."Rah chhuah nun." *El-Bethel Magazine* 3/26 (June, 1992): 2-9.

..........."Jacoba Pathian." *El-Bethel Magazine* 3/27 (July, 1992): 2-9.

..........."Kraws-Pathian thiltum." *El-Bethel Magazine* 3/28 (August, 1992): 2-8.

.... "Abrahama Pathian." *El-Bethel Magazine* 3/29 (September, 1992): 2-8.

............"Nang Malsawmna ni ang che." *El-Bethel Magazine* 4/31 (Nov., 1992): 2-8.

.........."Inremna leh Thianghlimna." *El-Bethel Magazine* 4/32 (Dec., 1992): 2-10.

........."Thu Hmanhmawh ber." *El-Bethel Magazine* 4/33 (January, 1993): 2-8.

........."Jakoba Khualzin Kawng." *El-Bethel Magazine* 4/34 (February, 1993): 2-12.

........."Chhiahhlawh College." *El-Bethel Magazine* 4/35 (March, 1993): 2-10.

.........."Baptisma." *El-Bethel Magazine* 4/36 (April, 1993): 2-9.

........."Thlarau Thianghlim Pawl Tharna."*El-Bethel Magazine* 4/37 (May, 1993): 2-6.

.... "Thlarau Rah." *El-Bethel Magazine* 4/38 (June, 1993): 2-8.

.... "Kristian Chhungkua." *El-Bethel Magazine* 4/39 (July, 1993): 2-9.

.... "Kraws- Pangpar Rimtui." *El-Bethel Magazine* 4/40 (August, 1993): 2-5.

.... "Thuruk Enkawl tu." *El-Bethel Magazine* 5/41 (September, 1993): 2-8.

.... "Mihring Mantu." *El-Bethel Magazine* 5/42 (October, 1993): 2-8.

.... "Pathian Hmangaihna." *El-Bethel Magazine* 5/43 (November, 1993): 2-7.

.... "Zawlnei Putar." *El-Bethel Magazine* 5/44 (December, 1993): 2-8.

.... "Lei Hringnun piah ram." *El-Bethel Magazine* 5/45 (January, 1994): 2-10.

.... "Jerusalem Thar." *El-Bethel Magazine* 5/46 (February, 1994): 2-8.

.... "Kros Thisen Remna." *El-Bethel Magazine* 5/47 (March, 1994): 2-7.

.... "Moriah Tlangah." *El-Bethel Magazine* 5/48 (April, 1994): 2-8.

.... "Kraws." *El-Bethel Magazine* 5/49 (May, 1994): 2-11.

.... "Krista Thuhretu Rinawm." *El-Bethel Magazine* 5/50 (June, 1994): 2-9.

.... "Saruak Nun." *El-Bethel Magazine* 6/51 (July, 1994): 2-7.

.... "I Tihduhdah Isua." *El-Bethel Magazine* 6/52 (August, 1994): 2-8.

.... "Lalpaa Lawmna." *El-Bethel Magazine* 6/53 (September, 1994): 2-8.

.... "Thuchah Hnuhnung." *El-Bethel Magazine* 6/54 (October, 1994): 2-8.

.... "Dan leh Khawngaihna." *El-Bethel Magazine* 6/55 (November, 1994): 2-8.

.... "Thih Thlamuanna." *El-Bethel Magazine* 6/56 (December, 1994): 2-6.

.... "Kalvari High Court." *El-Bethel Magazine* 6/57 (January, 1995): 2-7.

.... "Lalpa Siam Khawpui Thar." *El-Bethel Magazine* 6/58 (February, 1995): 2-9.

.... "Hnehna nun thuruk leh a Panna Kalkawng." *El-Bethel Magazine* 6/59 (March, 1995): 2-7.

.... "Tum Tlatna." *El-Bethel Magazine* 6/60 (April, 1995): 2-8.

.... "Minhriat reng nan hei hi ti thin rawh u." *El-Bethel Magazine* 6/60 (April, 1995): 14-17.

.... "In dam tlang em?" *El-Bethel Magazine* 7/61 (May, 1995): 2-7.

.... "Thlarau Chawlhna Isua." *El-Bethel Magazine* 7/62 (June, 1995): 2-8.

.... "Thlarau Thianghlim a lo thlenin." *El-Bethel Magazine* 7/63 (July, 1995): 2-9.

..........."Pathian Thuruk inthup puan chhuahna." *El-Bethel Magazine* 7/65 (September, 1995): 2-7.

.... "Zanriah Hnuhnung." *El-Bethel Magazine* 7/66 (October, 1995): 2-6.

.... "Damlai Tuipui Fawn Piah Lamah." *El-Bethel Magazine* 7/67 (November & December, 1995): 2-7.

.... "Retheite Lalpa." *El-Bethel Magazine* 7/68 (January, 1996): 2-4.

.... "Ral leh mai thin Lei Hring Nun." *El-Bethel Magazine* 7/69 (Feb., 1996): 2-8.

.... "Tuinung Lui." *El-Bethel Magazine* 7/70 (March, 1996): 2-7.

Lalnunthara, H. "El-Bethel Camp Report: Harangajao Buolmoul Bagan-II N.C. Hills Assam." *El-Bethel Magazine 7*/68 (January, 1996): 11-13.

"Lawngtlai El-Bethel ah Sakei leh Sakhị an tel ve tlat." *Forum* 1/23 (July 4-9, 1990): 2-3.

"Lawrkhawm."*Darthlalang*, Silver Jubilee Special Issue. (Aizawl: An Organ of Tuikual Branch KTP, 2005): 32.

Lentlang Weekly News 2/11 (March, 1990): 4

Lianthanga. K. "Rinna Thlai Chi Tuh." *Bethesda* (14 October, 1989).

Malsawma, J. "Testimony." *El-Bethel Magazine* 2/13 (May, 1991): 6-11.

"Mualpui El-Bethel Camp zawh ani." *Forum* 1/8 (April, 1990): 2.

Nampui, Thankhuma. "Fiangpui El-Bethel Report." *El-Bethel Magazine* 7/67 (November & December, 1995): 11-12.

Nang, Rev. G. K. "Testimony." *El-Bethel Magazine* 5/41 (September, 1993): 14.

Pa, Zorinkimi. "Bethel hi Engang in nge I Ngaih." *Sakeibaknei* 1/295 (Apr. 3, 1990): 4-5.

Pachuau, Lalsangkima. "Thlarau lama intodelh nan." *Kristian Tlangau* LXXX/959 (September, 1991): 19-22.

Pelkmann, Frank Kurschner. "Mizoram ka hmuh dan." *Kristian Tlangau* LXXIX/9969 (July, 1992): 23-24.

Pudaite, Lalpiangliana. "Bethel Report: Haflong." *El-Bethel Magazine* 7/65 (September, 1995): 8-11.

Raltawna, R. "Nazaret Isua a kal ani." *Zo Ni Eng*, 5/1 (January 17-24, 1990): 5.

"Rinna Thlai Chi (The Seed Faith). *El-Bethel Magazine* 2/20 (Dec., 1991): 11-12.

Robawiha, Rev. "Bethel-ah ka kal ve a." *Kristian Tlangau* LXXIX/950 (May, 1990): 11-15.

Rothangliani. "Testimony." *El-Bethel Magazine* 6/56 (December, 1994): 16-17.

Runia, Klaas. "Preaching and the Work of the Holy Spirit" part 2. *The Reformed Theological Review* 160/1 (April 2001): 30-41.

Sangzuala, C. "El-Bethel Thli." *Kristian Tlangau* LXXVIII/39 (February, 1990): 6.

........."Kum 1990 Mizoram." *Kristian Tlangau* LXXIX/950 (December, 1990): 29-32.

Shoute, Cin Za Do. "Damna Changa Lawmthu Sawina." *El-Bethel Magazine* 5/43 (November, 1993): 7.

Thanga, R.C. "El-Bethel ah ka kal ve." *Sakeibaknei* 4 /707 (November 9, 1990): 4-5.

"The letter to the Team Leader of El-Bethel Team from the Secretary El-Bethel Camp at Laisong (Naga village), Dated 24th February 1996." *El-Bethel Magazine* 7/70 (March, 1996): 8-9.

"Thingsai Pastor Bial El-Bethel Camp Report." *El-Bethel Magazine* 2/11 (February, 1991): 15.

Vaiphei, Tinting. "Testimony." *El-Bethel Magazine* 4/37 (May, 1993): 9-11.

"West Phaileng El-Bethel Camp." *El-Bethel Magazine* 2/11 (February, 1991): 16.

Books

Adams, Jay E. *Sermon Analysis.* Denver: Accent Publications, Inc., 1986.

Baumann, J. Daniel. *An Introduction to Contemporary Preaching.* Grand Rapids: Baker Book House, 1981.

Buttric, D. *Homiletic: Moves and Structure*. Philadelphia: Fortress Press, 1987.

Barth, Karl. *Evangelical Theology: An Introduction.* New York: Holt, Rinehart and Winston, 1963.

Cennick, Rev. J. (Translated by Rev. Liangkhaia "En rawh chhumzingah a lokal") No. 240. *Presbyterian Kohhran leh Mizoram Baptist Kohhran Kristian Hla Bu.* Aizawl: Synod Literature and Publication Board, 2004.

Cox, James W. "Evaluating the Sermon." *Hand Book of Contemporary Preaching*. Edited by Michael Duduit. Wheaton: Broadman Press, 1992, 225-235.

Chanmari Kohhran leh Khawtlang Chanchin: Mizoram Gospel Centenary Souvenir 1994. Aizawl: Chanmari Presbyterian Kohhran, 1993.

Chanmari Presbyterian Kohhran Golden Jubilee 1955-2005 Souvenir. Aizawl: Chanmari Presbyterian Church, 2005.

Cox, James W. *A Guide to Biblical Preaching.* Nashville: Abingdon, 1923.

Darthlalang Special Issue, Silver Jubilee. Aizawl: An Organ of Tuikual Branch KTP 2005.

Dawrpui Vengthar Pastor Bial Silver Jubilee 1969-1994 Souvenir. Aizawl: The Presbyterian Church of India Dawrpui Vengthar Pastor Bial, 1994.

Dawrpui Vengthar Presbyterian Kohhran Chanchin 1955-2000: New Millennium Souvenir. Aizawl: Dawrpui Vengthar Kohhran, 2001.

Davies, Horton. *Varieties of English Preaching 1900-1960*. London: SCM Press Ltd., 1963.

Demary, Donald E. *An Introduction to Homiletics*. Grand Rapids: Baker Book House, 1974.

Edwards, Brian H. *Revival! A People Saturated With God*. Darlington: Evangelical Press, 1990.

Forsyth, P. T. *Positive Preaching and the Modern Mind.* Michigan: Baker Book House, 1980.

Firth, C. B. *An Introduction to Indian Church History.* Delhi: ISPCK, 2001.

Habershon, Ada R. (Translated by Thanga, "Van hmun Ropui hmangaih ram khi"), No. 489. *Presbyterian Kohhran leh Mizoram Baptist Kohhran Kristian Hla Bu.*Aizawl: Synod Literature and Publication Board, 2004.

Harbour, Brian L. "Concluding the Sermon." *Hand Book of Contemporary Preaching.* Edited by Michael Duduit. Wheaton: Broadman Press, 1992, 225-235.

Isaiah, G. *Preach the Word: The Basics of Homiletics.* Tiruvalla: Christava Sahitya Samithi, 2004.

Laibata. "Kan velah Buh laktur tamtak a hminta e." No 390. *Presbyterian Kohhran leh Mizoram Baptist Kohhran Kristian Hla Bu.* Aizawl: Synod Literature and Publication Board, 2004.

Lalbiakmawia Rev, Dr. R. *Synod Department–te Inkaihhruaina.* Aizawl: Synod Multipurpose Training Centre, 2005.

Lalchhuangliana, Upa B. "Edenthar Presbyterian Kohhran Chanchin." *Mizoram Presbyterian Church Chanmari Pastor Bial Souvenir (1975-2000).* Aizawl: Chanmari Pastor Bial, 2000.

Lalhmangaiha, Upa R. "Chanmari Presbyterian Kohhran Chanchin." *Mizoram Presbyterian Church Chanmari Pastor Bial Souvenir (1975-2000).* Aizawl: Chanmari Pastor Bial, 2000.

Lalhmingliana, K. *El-Bethel Camp Sermon, Vol. I.* Aizawl: El-Publication Board, 1993.

Lalhmuaka. *Zoram Thim ata Engah.* Aizawl: Synod Publication Board,1988.

Lalnghinglova, Rev. *Zoram Nghahchhan.* Aizawl: Saikungi, 1993.

Lalhriatpuii, *Ka Damna Isua.* Aizawl: Bawlliana Mission Veng. 2004.

Lalrinnunga, Rev. F. "Synod Revival Committee Report." *Harhna Mizoram Revival*

Centenary Souvenir (1906-2006). Aizawl: Synod Revival Committee, 2006.

Lalsawma, Rev. *Kristian Thurin Zirna Bu (The Study of Christian Doctrine).* Aizawl: Synod Literature and Publication Board, 1998.

.........*Revivals the Mizo Way.* Aizawl: Lalsawma, Mission Vengthlang, 1994.

Liangkhaia. *Mizorama Harhna Thu.* Aizawl: LTL Publication, 2006.

Lischer, Richard. *A Theology of Preaching.* Nashville: Abingdon, 1981.

Macquarie, John. *Jesus Christ in Modern Thought.* London: SCM Press, 1990.

Mizoram Presbyterian Kohhran Department Chanchin. Aizawl: Synod Publication Board, 1987.

Ogilvie, Lloyd John. "Introducing the Sermon." *Hand Book of Contemporary Preaching.* Edited by Michael Duduit. Wheaton: Broadman Press, 1992, 175-187.

Pakunga, PC. "Chanmari West Presbyterian Kohhran Chanchin." *Mizoram Presbyterian Church Chanmari Pastor Bial Souvenir (1975-2000).* Aizawl: Chanmari Pastor Bial, 2000.

Perry, Lloyd M. & John R. Strubhar. *Evangelistic Preaching.* Chicago: Moody Press, 1979.

Prakash, Perumalla Surya. *The Preaching of Sadhu Sunder Singh.* Bangalore: Wordmakers, 1991.

Presbyterian Kohhran Aizawl Venglai Kum 10 tlin Lawmna Souvenir 1989-1999. Aizawl: Presbyterian Church, Aizawl Venglai, 1999.

Ralte, Upa Ramhmangaiha. "Dinthar Kohhran Chanchin." *Presbyterian Church of India: Dinthar: Aizawl Silver Jubilee Souvenir (15.8. 1976-15. 8. 2001).* Aizawl: Dinthar Presbyterian Kohhran, 2001.

Remthanga Rev. H. & Rev Lalbiaktluanga. *Kohhran Chanchin (1500-1990).* Aizawl: Synod Publication Board, 1990.

Rozika, Upa L. "Chanmari Pastor Bial Silver Jubilee (1975-2000)." *Mizoram Presbyterian Church Chanmari Pastor Bial Souvenir (1975-2000).* Aizawl: Chanmari Pastor Bial, 2000.

Ramnghinglova, Upa J. H. "Chanmari Pastor Bial Chanchin Tlangpui (1975-2000 AD)."*Mizoram Presbyterian Church Chanmari Pastor Bial Souvenir (1975-2000).* Aizawl: Chanmari Pastor Bial, 2000.

Sailo, K. Hawla. "El-Bethel Harhna." *Harhna: Mizoram Revival Centenary Souvenir (1906-2006).* Aizawl: Synod Revival Committee, 2006.

Sangster, W. E. *The Craft of the Sermon.* London: The Epworth Press, 1964.

Sogaard, Viggo. *Media in Church and Mission: Communicating the Gospel.* California: William Carey Library, 1993.

Steward, James S. *Heralds of God.* Michigan: Baker Book House, 1974.

Steward, William. *The Nature and Calling of the Church.* Madras: Christian Literature Society, 1958.

Stott, John R. W. *I Believe in Preaching.* London: Hodder and Stoughton, 1982.

Thanmawia, Upa Dr. R. L. ed. *Harhna Mizoram Revival Centenary Souvenir (1906-2006).* Aizawl: Synod Revival Committee, 2006.

The fifth Book of Synod Revival, Major Guidelines of Camp and Campaign, Mizoram Presbyterian Church. Aizawl: Synod Revival Committee, 2002.

The King James Version. Cambridge: Cambridge, 1769.

The New Revised Standard Version. Nashville, TN: Thomas Nelson Publishers, 1989.

Turnbull. Ralph G. ed. *Baker's Hand Book of Practical Theology.* Michigan: Baker Book House, 1967.

Vanlallawma, C. *Bethel Revival leh Lausanne Thuthlung.* Aizawl: Lengchhawn Press, 1990.

Vanlalchhuanawma. *Christianity and Subaltern Culture: Revival Movement as a Cultural Response to Westernization in Mizoram.* Madras: ISPCK, 2006.

Weber, Timothy P. "Revivals." *Concise Encyclopaedia of Preaching.* Edited by William H. Willimon and Richard Lischer. Louisville: Westminster John Knox Press, 1995: 406-409.

Zaikima, V. L. *Ka Tla Fai Ta: Bethel Harhna leh a Behbawm. Aizawl*: Lengchhawn Press, 1990.

Zalawma Rev. H & Rev. H. Vanlalruata. *An Introduction to Worship and Preaching*. Aizawl: Aizawl Theological College, 2005.

1976 Synod Bu. Aizawl: Synod Literature and Publication Board, 1977.

1978 Synod Bu. Aizawl: Synod Literature and Publication Board, 1979.

1987 Synod Bu. Aizawl: Synod Literature and Publication Board, 1988.

1988 Synod Bu. Aizawl: Synod Literature and Publication Board, 1989.

1989 Synod Bu. Aizawl: Synod Literature and Publication Board, 1990.

1990 Synod Bu. Aizawl: Synod Literature and Publication Board, 1991.

1991 Synod Bu. Aizawl: Synod Literature and Publication Board, 1992.

1992 Synod Bu. Aizawl: Synod Literature and Publication Board, 1993.

1993 Synod Bu. Aizawl: Synod Literature and Publication Board, 1994.

1994 Synod Bu. Aizawl: Synod Literature and Publication Board, 1995.

1995 Synod Bu. Aizawl: Synod Literature and Publication Board, 1996.

1996 Synod Bu. Aizawl: Synod Literature and Publication Board, 1997.

1997 Synod Bu. Aizawl: Synod Literature and Publication Board, 1998.

1998 Synod Bu. Aizawl: Synod Literature and Publication Board, 1999.

Unpublished Materials

Chanmari Pastorate Standing Committee Minute book of 1990. Mizoram Presbyterian Church.

Chuhveli, Camp Diary, 15th -18th January 1990.

Dawrpui Vengthar Pastorate Standing Committee Minute book of 1990, Mizoram Presbyterian Church.

Funeral video of K. Lalhmingliana, Speaker of El-Bethel Team, 20th May, 2004.

Lalhluna, Upa. Secretary of the Organizing Committee of El-Bethel Joint camp of the Chanmari and Dawrpui Vengthar Pastorates report to the author, 21st May, 2006.

Lalhmingliana, K. *El-Bethel Team Speaker K. Lalhmingliana Chanchin (Autobiography of K. Lalhmingliana)* Type and edited by Zohmangaiha of Chhinga Veng Aizawl on March, 6-8, 2001.

LaIsawma. "The Work of the Holy Spirit and Tribal Religious Emotionalism." M.Th. Thesis, Senate of Serampore College, 1968.

Lalthuama, C. *El- Bethel Camp Hla* (*The song of El-Bethel Camp*).

.... "El-Bethel atanga kan mize lan theihna te." (The appearance of our character through El-Bethel).

Minute of the 68th Synod Revival Committee on 17th. January, 1990.

Mizoram Presbyterian Church, Chhimphei Presbytery Meeting Minute of 1976.

Lalhmangaiha. "A Study of the Theology of Three Mizo Itinerant Evangelists in the Light of Pauline kerugma: An Evaluation" B.D. Thesis, Senate of Serampore College, 1997.

Synod Pastoral Committee Minute of 27 October, 1990, Aizawl, Mizoram.

The letter of K. Lalhmingliana, from Chhiahtlang on 18 June, 1995 to K. Hawla.

The letter of K. Lalhmingliana, from Champhai on 11 May, 1995 to K. Hawla.

The minute of the 40th sitting of The Luangmual Pastorate Standing Committee on 29th November, 1989.

The 8th Dawrpui Vengthar Pastorate Standing Committee Minute Book of 1989, Mizoram Presbyterian Church.

The 127th Chanmari Pastorate Standing Committee Minute Book of 1989, Mizoram Presbyterian Church.

The 128th Chanmari Pastorate Standing Committee Minute of 1989, Mizoram Presbyterian Church.

The 9th Dawrpui Vengthar Pastorate Standing Committee Minute Book of 1990, Mizoram Presbyterian Church.

Thanchhunga, Lal. "El-*Bethel leh Kei (My self and El-Bethel).*"

The Minute of the 130th Sitting of Chanmari Pastorate Standing Committee on 29th January, 1990.

The letter from Rev. Vanlalfaka S.E.S. i/c Revival, Synod Office, Dated 5th February, 2002.

The Minute of the 80th sitting of Synod Revival Committee on 14th June, 1991, Aizawl, Mizoram.

The Minute of the 117th Sitting of the Synod Revival Committee on 26th November, 1997, Aizawl, Mizoram.

The Minute of the 121st Sitting of the Synod Revival Committee on 28th October, 1998, Aizawl, Mizoram.

The Minute of the 131st sitting of Chanmari Pastorate Standing Committee on 3rd February, 1990.

The Minute of the 133rd Sitting of the Synod Revival Committee on 6th February, 2001, Aizawl, Mizoram.

The report of the study Team of Aizawl Theological College Faculty on Bethel Revival Movement, 1990.

Vanlaltluanga, R. "Revival movement in Mizoram with Special Reference to Bethel Revival: A theological Evaluation." B.D Thesis, Senate of Serampore College, 1997.

Zalawma. Rev. H. "The Role of Doctrinal Preaching in the Mizoram Presbyterian Church to Counter Sectarianism." M. Th. thesis, Senate of Serampore College, 1992.

Zoram Harhna Ropui - El-Bethel, Volume II.

Appendix-1

List of Interviewee

1. Mr. V. L. Zaikima on 27. 4. 2006 at Khatla
2. Mr. Rohmingliana on 27. 4. 2006 at Dawrpui
3. Upa. V. Neihkunga on 28. 4. 2006 at Chanmari
4. Mr. K. Hawla on 28. 4. 2006 at Tuikual
5. Mr. Thanchhunga on 28. 4. 2006 at Tuikual
6. Upa. R. Lallianzuala on 29. 4. 2006 at Chanmari
7. Mr. Lalbiakliana on 29. 4. 2006 at Chanmari
8. Upa. V.L. Ruata on 29. 4. 2006 at Chanmari
9. Rev. C. Laltanliana on 29. 4. 2006 at Chanmari
10. Mr. V. Lalliana on 30. 4. 2006 at Khatla
11. Upa. Lalliana on 3. 5. 2006 at Dinthar
12. Upa. C. Thansiama on 6. 5. 2006 at Chanmari West
13. Upa. Lalkunga on 6. 5. 2006 at Chanmari West
14. Upa. Hmingthanga on 6. 5. 2006 at Electric Veng
15. Upa. J. H. Ramnghinglova on 7. 5. 2006 at Chanmari
16. Upa. C. Thanseia on 12. 5. 2006 at Chanmari
17. Mr. Rozinga on 12. 5. 2006 at Chanmari

18. Mrs. Lianzuali on 12. 5.2006 at Chanmari
19. Mrs. Chuhveli on 12. 5. 2006 at Chanmari
20. Upa. Lalhluna on 12. 5. 2006 at Vaivakawn
21. Upa. Lalkhawhluna on 12. 5. 2006 at Dawrpui Vengthar
22. Rev. C. Vanlalhruaia on 13. 5. 2006 at Ramhlun 'S'
23. Mr. Zorammawia on 14. 5. 2006 at Laipuitlang
24. Mr. B. Lalbiakthuama on 14. 5. 2006 at Laipuitlang
25. Mr. Sangliana on 15. 5. 2006 at Chanmari
26. Dr. Zokhuma on 17. 5. 2006 at Chanmari
27. Upa. Lalhrangluaia on 17. 5. 2006 at Chanmari
28. Mrs. Lalhriatpuii on 17. 5. 2006 at Mission Veng
29. Mrs. Lalsupuii on 18. 5. 2006 at Dinthar
30. Mr. Vanneihtluanga on 19. 5. 2006 at Chanmari
31. Mrs. Thawmliani Wife of. K. Lalhmingliana on 19. 5. 2006 at Champhai.
32. Mr. Khiangthuama Son of K. Lalhmingliana on 19. 5. 2006 at Champhai
33. Mr. Ramdinzauva Son of K. Lalhmingliana on 19. 5. 2006 at Champhai
34. Mr. K Chanchinmawia Son of K. Lalhmingliana on 19. 5. 2006 at Champhai
35. Mrs. Laldinthari Daughter of K. Lalhmingliana on 19. 5. 2006 at Champhai
36. Upa. Dohmingthanga on 21. 5. 2006 at Aizawl Venglai
37. Upa. R. Lalrawna on 21. 5. 2006 at Aizawl Venglai
38. Upa. Rozara on 21. 5. 2006 at Aizawl Venglai
39. Rev. S. R. Lalkailuaia on 26. 5. 2006 at Dinthar
40. Mr. C. Lalthuama on 28. 5. 2006 at Bungkawn

Appendix-2

El-Bethel Counselling

1. Themes in the Counselling Class

The camp programme contains counselling class which is very significant for self evaluation for the campers. Mass-counselling type was used since many people were there in the Camp. The following topics were used regularly in every El-Bethel Camp:

1. The Two Hills
2. Contentment in Every Aspect John 19:11, Romans 8:28, Lamentation 3:27-41, Job1:12; 2:6 Psalm 121:3-8.
3. Are you saved? Matthew 1:21
4. Mr. Vana and Miss. Siami. Songs of Solomon 5:2-8
5. Two Types of Resurrection. John 11:44, 20:6-7
6. The Captive Life. Psalm 137
7. Salvation: God is pleased in the Blood of Jesus. I Thessalonians 1:5-6.
8. Faith and offering Hebrew 1:1, Isaiah 53:1-2.
9. The good and bad. Philippians 2:13
10. The life of Philemon.1-25

2. The Themes and Biblical References in the Counselling Class at Tanhril Camp

There were seven times for mass counselling in Tanhril Gospel camp. The following themes and Biblical references were used (Pi. Chuhveli Camp Diary (unpublished). All the themes have Biblical texts except 'The Two Hills.'

Table: Timetable of Counselling class in the El-bethel camp at Tanhril

Date	Time	Theme.	Biblical References
15. 1. 1990	6:30-9:00PM	Salvation: God is Pleased in the Blood of Jesus.	I Thessalonians. 1: 5-6.

Date (Wed)	Time	Theme	Biblical References
16.1.1990	7 -9:00AM	The Captive life	Psalm 137.
	11:30-1:00PM	Two Types of Resurrection	John 11:44, Col. 3:5-10
	2-4:00 PM	Faith and Offering.	Heb. 1:1, Isaiah 53:1-2.
	6:30-9:00, PM	Contentment in Every Aspect	Rom. 8:28-29, Job. 1:12, 2: 6.

Date	Time	Theme	Biblical References
17.1.1990	7 -9:00AM	Good and Bad	Philippi 2:13
	11:30-1:00PM	The Two Hills	
	2-3:00 PM	The life of Philemon: Character Study	Philemon 1-25

Appendix-3

The Sermons of K. Lalhmingliana, Themes and Biblical References

1. Tlawmna nun- Misualte hnen thlengphak Chanchin Tha (Humility-The Gospel that Reaches Sinners). Luke 5:29-32, 10:30-35, 19: 5-7.[633]
2. Khawvel Tukverh (The Window to the World). II Samuel 11:1-13.[634]
3. Taitea tel lovin (Without the Lad). Genesis 44:30-34, Proverb 22:6, 24:11.[635]
4. Tuihna Kang Ngailo Nun (The Life of a never ending Fountain). Isaiah 58:6-12.[636]

---

633 K. Lalhmingliana, "Tlawmna nun- Misualte hnen thlengphak Chanchin Tha," *El-Bethel Magazine*, No. I, (April 1990): 9-12, K. Lalhmingliana, *El-Bethel Camp Sermon* 1/I (Aizawl: El-Publication Board, 1993), 1-7.

634 K. Lalhmingliana, "Khawvel Tukverh," *El-Bethel Magazine*, 1/2 (May 1990): 3-7; K. Lalhmingliana, *El-Bethel Camp Sermon* ..., 101-110.

635 K. Lalhmingliana, "Taitea tel lovin," *El-Bethel Magazine*, 1/3 (June 1990): 2-8; K. Lalhmingliana, *El-Bethel Camp Sermon* ..., 90-100.

636 K. Lalhmingliana, "Tuihna Kang Ngailo Nun," *El-Bethel Magazine*, 1/4 (July 1990): 3-13; K. Lalhmingliana, *El-Bethel Camp Sermon* ..., 62-79.

5. Thlamuanna duh lo nun (The Life that Negates Comforts). Psalm 77:1-4, Matthew 7:42[637]
6. Kros Hmelma (Enemy of the Cross). Philippians 3:17-20.[638]
7. Puan In zauh (Extending the Tent). Isaiah 54:1-3.[639]
8. Remna Lal (Prince of Peace). Isaiah 9:6-7.[640]
9. Mitinin an Chhiara chu (The Life Read by All). II Corinthians 3:2-6, Habakkuk 2: 2.[641]
10. Kraws Fate Kalkawng (The Path of the Children of the Cross). Psalm 84:1-7.[642]
11. Kristian Nun: Boralna Chihnih (The Christian Life: Two Ways to Ruin). Genesis 19:15-17.[643]
12. Kros Pathian Thiltihtheihlohna (Cross, the Powerlessness of God). I Corinthians 1:18-18.[644]
13. Pathian Ruai Ropui (The Great Banquet of God). Revelation 19:17-18, Matthew 28:8-10. John 6:48-58, Luke 22:19-20, I Corinthians 11:26[645]

---

637 K. Lalhmingliana, "Thlamuanna duh lo nun," *El-Bethel Magazine*, 1/6 (September 1990): 2-7; K. Lalhmingliana, *El- Bethel Camp Sermon* ..., 120-130.

638 K. Lalhmingliana, "Kros Hmelma," *El-Bethel Magazine*, 1/7, (October 1990): 2-6; K. Lalhmingliana, *El-Bethel Camp Sermon* ..., 140-147.

639 K. Lalhmingliana, "Puan In zauh," *El-Bethel Magazine*,1/8, (November 1990): 2-8; K. Lalhmingliana, *El-Bethel Camp Sermon* ..., 80-89.

640 K. Lalhmingliana, "Remna Lal," *El-Bethel Magazine*, 1/9, (December 1990): 2-7; K. Lalhmingliana, *El-Bethel Camp Sermon* ..., 198-207.

641 K. Lalhmingliana, "Mitinin an Chhiara chu," *El-Bethel Magazine*, 2/11, (February 1991): 2-11; K. Lalhmingliana, *El-Bethel Camp Sermon* ..., 8- 24.

642 K. Lalhmingliana, "Kraws Fate Kalkawng," *El-Bethel Magazine*, 2/12, (March & April 1991): 2-9; K. Lalhmingliana, *El-Bethel Camp Sermon* ..., 157-167.

643 K. Lalhmingliana, "Kristian Nun: Boralna Chihnih," *El-Bethel Magazine*, 2/13, (May 1991): 2-6; K. Lalhmingliana, *El-Bethel Camp Sermon* ..., 131-139.

644 K. Lalhmingliana, "Kros Pathian Thiltihtheihlohna," *El-Bethel Magazine*, 2/15, (July 1991): 2-7; K. Lalhmingliana, *El- Bethel Camp Sermon* ..., 148-156.

645 K. Lalhmingliana, "Pathian Ruai Ropui," *El-Bethel Magazine*, 2/16, (August 1991); 4-10; K. Lalhmingliana, *El-Bethel Camp Sermon* ..., 187-197.

14. Tinungtu Thlarau Thianghlim (Holy Spirit the giver of Life). John 6:63.[646]
15. Penticost Thlarau Thiltum (The aim of the Pentecost Spirit). John 20:21-23.[647]
16. Saltang nun (The Captive life). Psalm 137:1-6, Colossians 3:15[648]
17. I Ram lo Thleng Rawh se (Thy Kingdom come). Matthew 6:9-14.[649]
18. A Lokal lehna (The Second Coming). Luke 21:34-36.[650]
19. Tibotu Thinlung na (The painful heart of the loser). Luke 15:1-2.[651]
20. Mupui ang Kohhran Thianghlim (The Holy Church like an Eagle). Deut.32:9-13.[652]
21. Khandaih hriam tawn (Two edged Sword). Hebrew 4:12.[653]
22. Pathian Indona (The War of God).II Chronicles 20:12, 15, II Corinthians 10:3-6.[654]

---

646 K. Lalhmingliana, " Tinungtu Thlarau Thianghlim," *El-Bethel Magazine*, 2/17, (September 1991): 2-7; K. Lalhmingliana, *El- Bethel Camp Sermon* ..., 25-43.

647 K. Lalhmingliana, "Penticost Thlarau Thiltum," *El-Bethel Magazine*, 2/18, (October 1991): 2-8.

648 K. Lalhmingliana, "Saltang nun," *El-Bethel Magazine*, 2/19, (November 1991): 1-5; K. Lalhmingliana, *El- Bethel Camp Sermon* ..., 111-119. Zoram Harhna Ropui - El-Bethel, Volume II (unpublished).

649 K. Lalhmingliana, "I Ram lo Thleng Rawh se," El-Bethel Magazine, 2/19, (November 1991): 6-10; *Zoram Harhna Ropui II* (unpublished).

650 K. Lalhmingliana, "A Lokal lehna," *El-Bethel Magazine*, 2/20, (December 1991): 2-10.

651 K. Lalhmingliana, "Tibotu Thinlung na," *El Bethel Magazine*, 3/21, (January 1992): 2-6.

652 K. Lalhmingliana, "Mupui ang Kohhran Thianghlim," El-Bethel Magazine, 3/22,(February 1992): 2-6; *Zoram Harhna Ropui II* (unpublished).

653 K. Lalhmingliana, "Khandaih hriam tawn," *El-Bethel Magazine*, 3/23, (March 1992): 5-10; *Zoram Harhna Ropui II* (unpublished).

654 K. Lalhmingliana, "Pathian Indona," *El-Bethel Magazine*, 3/23, (March 1992): 10-14.

23. Pathian Thuawih (Obedience to God). Deuteronomy 21:18-21.[655]
24. Tho ila, Bethel-ah I kal ang u (Let's rise and go to Bethel). Genesis 35:1-5, Jeremiah 17:10.[656]
25. Krista a Kan Nihna (Our Nature in Christ). Colossians1:13, 19; 2:14; 3:1, Ephesians 2:1-6.[657]
26. Rah chhuah nun (the Fruit bearing Life). Ezekiel 11:19-21, John 15:5-18.[658]
27. Jacoba Pathian (The God of Jacob). Herew 2:11-12, 21; Exodus 3:6.[659]
27. Kraws-Pathian thiltum (Cross-the Purpose of God). Genesis 3:15.[660]
29. Abrahama Pathian (The God of Abraham). Genesis 22:1-2.[661]
30. Nang Malsawmna ni ang che (Be a blessing). Isaiah 35:3; 58:6-7; Genesis12:2[662]
31. Inremna leh Thianghlimna (Holiness and Harmony). Hebrew 12:14[663]

---

655 K. Lalhmingliana, "Pathian Thuawih," *El-Bethel Magazine*, 3/24, (April 1992): 6-11.

656 K. Lalhmingliana, "Tho ila, Bethel-ah I kal ang u," *El-Bethel Magazine*, 3/25, (May 1992): 2-7; K. Lalhmingliana, *El- Bethel Camp Sermon* ..., 233-242.

657 K. Lalhmingliana, "Krista a Kan Nihna," *El-Bethel Magazine*, 3/25, (May 1992):8-12; *Zoram Harhna Ropui II* (unpublished).

658 K. Lalhmingliana, "Rah chhuah nun," *El-Bethel Magazine*, 3/26, (June1992): 2-9; *Zoram Harhna Ropui II* (unpublished).

659 K. Lalhmingliana, "Jacoba Pathian," *El-Bethel Magazine*, 3/27, (July 1992): 2-9.

660 K. Lalhmingliana, "Kraws- Pathian thiltum," El-*Bethel Magazine*, 3/28, (August 1992): 2-8.

661 K. Lalhmingliana, "Abrahama Pathian," *El-Bethel Magazine*, 3/29, (September 1992): 2-8; K. Lalhmingliana, El-Bethel Camp Sermon ..., 225-232.

662 K. Lalhmingliana, "Nang Malsawmna ni ang che," *El-Bethel Magazine*, 4/31, (November 1992): 2-8.

663 K. Lalhmingliana, "Inremna leh Thianghlimna," *El-Bethel Magazine*, 4/32, (December 1992): 2-10.

32. Thu Hmanhmawh ber (The Most Urgent Word). Matthew 28:18-20.[664]
33. Jakoba Khualzin Kawng (The Pilgrims of Jacob). Genesis 47:9.[665]
34. Chhiahhlawh College (The College of Servants). Isaiah 52:13-14.[666]
35. Baptism. Mark 16:15-16.[667]
36. Thlarau Thianghlim Pawl Tharna (The Fresh fellowship of the Holy Spirit). Ephesians 2:1-6, Colossians 1:19-22, I Corinthians 6:9-11.[668]
37. Thlarau Rah (The Fruit of the Spirit). The Song of Solomon 4:16.[669]
38. Kristian Chhungkua (Christian Family). Ephesians 5:33; I Corinthians 7:3, 5.[670]
39. Kraws-Pangpar Rimtui (Cross-the Aroma of the Flower). I Corinthians 1:18-19.[671]
40. Thuruk Enkawl tu (The Custodian of the Secret Word). I Corinthians 4:1-2, I John 2:15, James 4:4.[672]
41. Mihring Mantu (Fisher of Men). Luke 5:8-10, Matthew 16:13-15, Mark 1:16[673]

---

664 K. Lalhmingliana, "Thu Hmanhmawh ber," *El-Bethel Magazine*, 4/33, (January 1993): 2-8; K. Lalhmingliana, *El- Bethel Camp Sermon* ..., 215-224.

665 K. Lalhmingliana, "Jakoba Khualzin Kawng," *El-Bethel Magazine*,4/34, (February 1993): 2-12; *Zoram Harhna Ropui II.* (unpublished).

666 K. Lalhmingliana, "Chhiahhlawh College," *El-Bethel Magazine*, 4/35, (March 1993): 2-10.

667 K. Lalhmingliana, "Baptisma," *El-Bethel Magazine*, 4/36, (April 1993): 2-9.

668 K. Lalhmingliana, "Thlarau Thianghlim Pawl Tharna," *El-Bethel Magazine*, 4/37, (May 1993): 2-6; *Zoram Harhna Ropui II* (unpublished).

669 K. Lalhmingliana, "Thlarau Rah," *El-Bethel Magazine*, 4/38, (June 1993): 2-8.

670 K. Lalhmingliana, "Kristian Chhungkua," *El-Bethel Magazine*, 4/39, (July 1993): 2-9; *Zoram Harhna Ropui II* (unpublished).

671 K. Lalhmingliana, "Kraws-Pangpar Rimtui," *El-Bethel Magazine*, 4/40, (August 1993): 2-5.

672 K. Lalhmingliana, "Thuruk Enkawl tu," *El-Bethel Magazine*, 5/41, (September 1993): 2-8; *Zoram Harhna Ropui II* (unpublished).

673 K. Lalhmingliana, "Mihring Mantu," *El-Bethel Magazine*, 5/42, (October 1993): 2-8.

42. Pathian Hmangaihna (The Love of God). John 3:16, 17, 14:21, I John 3:16-18, Philemon 17-19.[674]
43. Zawlnei Putar (The Old Prophet). Isaiah 30:21[675]
44. Lei Hringnun piah ram (The Life beyond). Romans 12:1-2.[676]
45. New Jerusalem: Revelation Chapter 7, 21, 22[677]
46. Kros Thisen Remna (The Blood of Cross for Reconciliation). Leviticus 7:1[678]
47. Moriah Tlangah (On the Mount of Moreh). Genesis 22:1-2[679]
48. The Cross. I Corinthians 1:18[680]
49. Krista Thuhretu Rinawm (the Faithful Witnesses of Christ). I Corinthians 4:1-2, I John 2:15, James 4: 4.[681]
50. Saruak Nun (The Naked Life). Genesis 2:25[682]
51. I Tihduhdah Isua (I Am Jesus Whom You Persecuted). Acts 9:3-6[683]
52. Lalpaa Lawmna (Rejoicing in the Lord).Habakkuk 3:17-18[684]

---

674 K. Lalhmingliana, "Pathian Hmangaihna," *El-Bethel Magazine*, 5/43, (November 1993): 2-7.

675 K. Lalhmingliana, "Zawlnei Putar," *El-Bethel Magazine*, 5/44, (December 1993): 2-8.

676 K. Lalhmingliana, "Lei Hringnun piah ram," *El-Bethel Magazine*, 5/45, (January 1994): 2-10.

677 K. Lalhmingliana, "Jerusalem Thar," *El-Bethel Magazine*, 5/46, (February 1994): 2-8.

678 K. Lalhmingliana, "Kros Thisen Remna," *El-Bethel Magazine*, 5/47, (March 1994): 2-7.

679 K. Lalhmingliana, "Moriah Tlangah," *El-Bethel Magazine*, 5/48, (April 1994): 2-8.

680 K. Lalhmingliana, "Kraws," *El-Bethel Magazine*, 5/49, (May 1994): 2-11.

681 K. Lalhmingliana, "Krista Thuhretu Rinawm," *El-Bethel Magazine*, 5/50, (June 1994): 2-9.

682 K. Lalhmingliana, "Saruak Nun," *El-Bethel Magazine*, 6/51, (July 1994): 2-7; *Zoram Harhna Ropui II* (unpublished).

683 K. Lalhmingliana, "I Tihduhdah Isua," *El-Bethel Magazine*, 6/52, (August 1994): 2-8.

684 K. Lalhmingliana, "Lalpaa Lawmna," *El-Bethel Magazine*, 6/53, (September 1994): 2-8; *Zoram Harhna Ropui II* (unpublished).

53. Thuchah Hnuhnung (The Last Will). Matthew 28:19-20[685]
54. Dan leh Khawngaihna (Law and Grace). Romans 10:5, Galatians 3:24[686]
55. Thih Thlamuanna (Peace In Death). Hebrew 9:27[687]
56. The High Court of Calvary. Isaiah 53:6[688]
57. Lalpa Siam Khawpui Thar (The New Created City of Lord). Revelation 21:1-4.[689]
58. Hnehna nun thuruk leh a Panna Kalkawng (the Secret and the Path to the Victorious Life).[690]
59. Tum Tlatna (Concrete Determination). Daniel 1:18[691]
60. Minhriat reng nan hei hi ti thin rawh u (Do this in Remembrance of me). I Corinthians 11: 23-26.[692]
61. In dam tlang em? (Are you doing all Right?). Ezekiel 39:18; 47: 9-10.[693]
62. Thlarau Chawlhna Isua (Jesus: the Resting Place of the Soul). Matthew 11:28-30.[694]

---

685 K. Lalhmingliana, "Thuchah Hnuhnung," *El-Bethel Magazine*, 6/54, (October 1994): 2-8.

686 K. Lalhmingliana, "Dan leh Khawngaihna," *El-Bethel Magazine*, 6/55, (November 1994): 2-8; *Zoram Harhna Ropui II* (unpublished).

687 K. Lalhmingliana, "Thih Thlamuanna," *El-Bethel Magazine*, 6/56, (December 1994): 2-6.

688 K. Lalhmingliana, "Kalvari High Court," *El-Bethel Magazine*, 6/57, (January 1995). 2-7. *Zoram Harhna Ropui II* (unpublished).

689 K. Lalhmingliana, "Lalpa Siam Khawpui Thar," *El-Bethel Magazine*, 6/58, (February 1995): 2-9.

690 K. Lalhmingliana, "Hnehna nun thuruk leh a Panna Kalkawng," *El-Bethel Magazine*, 6/59, (March 1995): 2-7.

691 K. Lalhmingliana, "Tum Tlatna," *El-Bethel Magazine*, 6/60, (April 1995): 2-8; Zoram Harhna Ropui II (unpublished).

692 K. Lalhmingliana, "Minhriat reng nan hei hi ti thin rawh u," *El-Bethel Magazine*, 6/60, (April 1995): 14-17.

693 K. Lalhmingliana, "In dam tlang em?," El-Bethel Magazine, 7/61, (May1995): 2-7; Zoram Harhna Ropui II (unpublished).

694 K. Lalhmingliana, "Thlarau Chawlhna Isua," *El-Bethel Magazine*, 7/62, (June 1995): 2-8.

63. Thlarau Thianghlim a lo thlenin (When the Holy Spirit Arrives). Ezekiel 11:19-21.[695]
64. Pathian Thuruk inthup Puan chhuahna (The Proclamation of the Secret Word of God). Hebrew 1:1-2.[696]
65. Zanriah Hnuhnung (The Last Supper). Luke 22:9-12.[697]
66. Damlai Tuipui Fawn Piah Lamah (Beyond the Troubled Sea of Life). Psalm 42:7[698]
67. Retheite Lalpa (The Lord of the Poor). Psalm 116:15, Exodus 22:22-27, Psalm 82:3-4.[699]
68. Ral leh mai thin Lei Hring Nun (the Ever Vanishing Life of the World). Job 14:1-2; II Corinthians 6: 2.[700]
69. Tuinung Lui (The Living Water). Ezekiel 47: 8-11.[701]
70. Counselling Kohhran (Counselling Church).[702]

---

695 K. Lalhmingliana, "Thlarau Thianghlim a lo thlenin," *El-Bethel Magazine*, 7/63, (July 1995): 2-9.

696 K. Lalhmingliana, "Pathian Thuruk inthup Puan chhuahna," *El-Bethel Magazine*, 7/65, (September 1995): 2-7; *Zoram Harhna Ropui II* (unpublished).

697 K. Lalhmingliana, "Zanriah Hnuhnung," *El-Bethel Magazine*, 7/66, (October 1995): 2-6.

698 K. Lalhmingliana, "Damlai Tuipui Fawn Piah Lamah," *El-Bethel Magazine*, 7/67, (November & December 1995): 2-7.

699 K. Lalhmingliana, "Retheite Lalpa," *El-Bethel Magazine*, 7/68, (January 1996): 2-4.

700 K. Lalhmingliana, "Ral leh mai thin Lei Hring Nun," *El-Bethel Magazine*, 7/69, (February 1996): 2-8; *Zoram Harhna Ropui II* (unpublished).

701 K. Lalhmingliana, "Tuinung Lui," *El-Bethel Magazine*, 7/70, (March 1996): 2-7.

702 K. Lalhmingliana, "Counselling Kohhran," *El-Bethel Magazine*, 2/14, (June 1991): 4-14; K. Lalhmingliana, *El- Bethel Camp Sermon* ..., 44-61.

Appendix-4

Table, Showing the Growth Rate of Chanmari and Dawrpui Vengthar Pastorates Offering from 1987-1997.

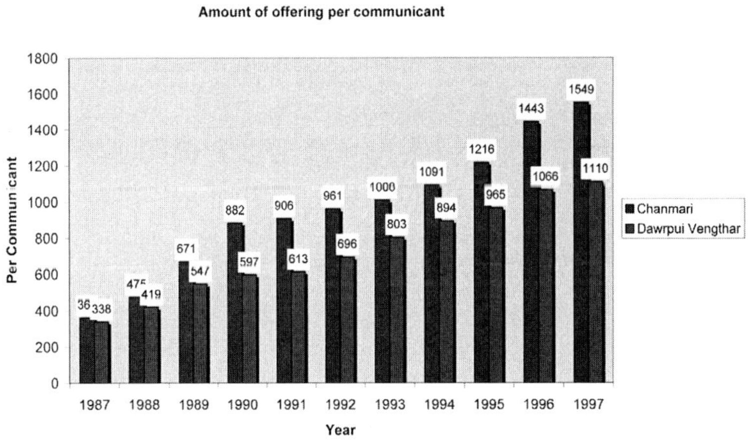